PAUL KALBURGI

Paul Kalburgi is a British playwright, screenwriter and television producer. He was awarded Master of Arts (Writing for Screen & Stage) in 2015 by Regent's University, London.

Select playwriting credits include *Broadway or Bust* (Bath House Cultural Center, Dallas), *In the Tall Grass* (Bishop Arts Theatre Center, Dallas; winner of 'Outstanding New Play' DFW Theater Critics Forum), *Maxine* (Stockwell Playhouse, London and Times Square Art Center, New York), *Almost The Birthday Party* (Etcetera Theatre, London; published by Lazy Bee Scripts), *MCN TV* (Brockley Jack Theatre, London), *Tickled Pink!* (Battersea Barge, London), *Jack & The Beanstalk* (touring, UK and Ireland), and *The Countess* (Blue Elephant Theatre, London).

Select screenwriting credits include *Shortland Street* (TVNZ, New Zealand), *The Price of Fame* (REELZ Channel, USA) and *Healing* (Revelation TV, UK; winner of 'Best Song' (music and lyrics) Concrete Dream Film Festival, Los Angeles). For television, Paul has produced programmes for a host of networks in the UK and USA since 2007, working across genres including celebrity ob-doc, docudrama, lifestyle, factual entertainment and news.

Alongside his writing projects, Paul continues to facilitate writing courses and workshops in the USA, UK and New Zealand. Paul is a proud member of the Dramatists Guild of America.

www.paulkalburgi.com

@PaulKalburgi

Paul Kalburgi

THE WRITER'S TOOLKIT

Exercises, Techniques and Ideas
for Playwrights and Screenwriters

NICK HERN BOOKS
London
www.nickhernbooks.co.uk

A Nick Hern Book

THE WRITER'S TOOLKIT

First published in Great Britain in 2020
by Nick Hern Books Limited
The Glasshouse, 49a Goldhawk Road,
London W12 8QP

Cover image: © Shutterstock.com/Sergey Korkin

Designed and typeset by Nick Hern Books, London
Printed and bound in Great Britain by
CPI Group (Ltd), Croydon CR0 4YY

A CIP catalogue record for this book
is available from the British Library

ISBN   978 1 84842 863 8

MIX
Paper from
responsible sources
FSC® C013604

For my boys,
Lohit, Zane and Zeven

Dream big. Who said you can't have it all?

'Twenty years from now you will be more disappointed
by the things you didn't do than by the ones you did.
So throw off the bowlines. Sail away from the safe harbour.
Catch the trade winds in your sails.
Explore. Dream. Discover.'

Mark Twain

CONTENTS

INTRODUCTION

'Procrastination is the thief of time.'

Edward Young

American playwright James Thurber once said, *'Don't get it right, get it written.'* A productive motto, which I try to keep in mind whenever I sit down to write, and something I always share with fellow writers in my classes and workshops. Just as an Olympic athlete must push through the pain barrier to achieve success on the track, writers must push past 'writer's block' to achieve success on the page – especially when inspiration is fleeting. Sometimes, this is easier said than done, of course. Writing is a creative process, which I believe can't be forced, so how do we keep writing and remain productive, when we are in a slump?

If a script is beginning to feel forced or sluggish, or you find yourself unable to write through or around a roadblock for lack of motivation or ideas, I suggest stepping back from 'scriptwriting' and refocus your creativity by simply 'writing'. Remove the confines of structure, story beats, and the pressure to produce work that needs to be 'good enough' to one day share with others (hopefully an audience), and allow yourself to indulge in the craft of writing. Discover how writing exercises and prompts can free you of expectation, judgement and the need to deliver. Sometimes we all need to throw a little sand outside of the sandbox, colour outside of the lines, and give ourselves permission to make a mess, in order to inspire real creativity.

If you are on a roll, however, and just need a little help to shape, improve or invigorate a scene, then a related writing exercise can help to highlight any sticking points and may suggest a new way forward. In this book I will share specific activities for the critical elements of scriptwriting, which will allow you to fine-tune your script and inspire new ideas.

Perhaps you are looking for inspiration for a new piece of writing? I have included 101 quick-fire writing prompts, so set a timer and get to it. There are no rules, just read the scenario, pick up a pen or open your laptop – and start writing. It's amazing how satisfying it can be to create a series of short, complete scenes in a brief amount of time, and this can provide a positive start to your writing session.

In this practical guide, I will share with you a bounty of original writing exercises and activities, as well as my riffs on some classics. Also included is an introduction to immersive writing and meditative writing. The latter is something that I have found hugely beneficial for the heart, mind and soul at the start and end of a writing session. Included are three mindful meditation exercises to try before your writing sessions, and a relaxing Savasana to finish your practice. I hope you will enjoy exploring the creative and spiritual benefits of meditative writing and find it a productive and enriching addition to your process.

The exercises in this book can be applied to any work-in-progress or used as a jumping-off point for a new piece of work. I hope that playwrights and screenwriters of all levels, including those who are new to the craft, will find them both refreshing and inspiring.

HOW TO USE THIS BOOK

'Fill your paper with the breathings of your heart.'

William Wordsworth

This book is divided into eight parts, each designed to help with a different part of the writing process. Writing is essentially an art form, not a science, and so the rules, devices and pointers given are provided as a guide and are not intended to stifle your creativity. As such, not every exercise will be relevant to every script, nor every writer, so run with the exercises which speak to you and feel free to adapt others to best serve your purpose.

Part 1 provides a collection of **mindful meditations**, created to provide a sense of calm and relaxation as a precursor to a productive writing session. Each one is roughly five minutes long and I hope that introducing these into your daily writing practice will make a positive difference to your day.

Part 2 offers a selection of **warm-up exercises**, designed to make sure your writing muscles are limber and to switch your creative mind to writing mode. The exercises in this part are shorter than the rest and are great to do without the thought or focus of applying them to a bigger piece of writing. They are quick and inspiring – great for those days when you don't have time to work on your current writing projects but still want to stay productive.

Part 3 is the largest section of the book, including exercises based around the fundamental elements of writing for stage and screen. These include **character**-based exercises, techniques for improving **dialogue**, how to include **subtext** in your writing, giving your scripts a strong sense of place or **setting**, as well as useful **plot** devices to heighten drama and raise the stakes.

Part 4 explores **immersive writing** techniques. See how you can lift the world of your script off the page and bring it into your writing space, to shape and mould in a physical sense. Similarly, it explains how you can physically enter the world of your script. Physical experiences and the use of props can add additional layers of texture to your writing.

Part 5 looks at how to master the **ten-minute play**. With so many playwriting competitions and festivals offering opportunities to get your work on stage and in front of an audience, a solid ten-minute play is a good thing to have in your arsenal. Ten-minute plays demonstrate lean and economical writing, and are great to attach to an email when reaching out to agents or industry professionals, and for building your writing resume.

Part 6 will help you to examine your work, making sure it's in great shape for sharing and submitting. The **submission surgery** provides exercises for fine-tuning your dialogue, scrutinising your scenes and also looks at the importance of hearing them off the page.

Writing prompts offer an inspiring jumping-off point from which to write a short scene. **Part 7** offers 101 **writing prompts**. Why not try a new one every day before you sit down to work on your current project? They are so easy, you could even do one whilst travelling to work, or waiting for the barista to make your latte.

Part 8 rewards a productive writing session with a little self-care. Just as mindful meditations are a great way to begin a writing session, practising **Savasana** is a wonderful way to relax and replenish the body, mind and soul when you have given so much to advancing your work. Savasana, or 'corpse pose' is simple to perform and provides balance whilst releasing stress.

If you have cleared out a day in your diary to dedicate to writing, you might include the exercises in this book and plan your day like this…

- Begin with a mindful meditation from Part 1.

- Warm up your writing muscle with an exercise from Part 2.

- Work on your own writing project, dipping into exercises from Part 3 if you need any pointers on character, dialogue, subtext, setting or plot.

- After lunch, why not try a quick writing prompt from Part 7 to re-energise your mind before returning to your project.

- Close your writing session with Savasana (Part 8), thanking yourself for all you have achieved.

All of the exercises in this book are designed to be done solo; however, many would be great to try out whilst working alongside fellow writers. I would encourage all writers to consider joining a local writers' group (if one doesn't exist, why not start one up?), where you can meet regularly to chat about your latest project, share tips and tricks, circulate news of writing opportunities, and find supportive and encouraging readers for your early drafts. If groups aren't your thing, consider finding a writing buddy. Just like having a friend to go to the gym with, find someone to check in with once a week, keeping each other focused and on track towards achieving your writing goals and deadlines. If you can't meet regularly in person, this could even be a weekly phone call.

Only you know the best way to tell your story. *Go write it!*

Here is a list of the tools that would be helpful to have at hand as you try out the exercises in this book:

- A towel or yoga mat (for Parts 1 and 8).

- A notebook and some scrap paper.

- Large sheets of paper, or a roll of wallpaper you can write on the back of.

- Post-it notes or index cards and mounting putty.

- Highlighters, marker pens, pens and pencils.

- A Dictaphone or mobile phone you can record audio on.

- A newspaper or magazine.

See *The Writing Space* on page 160 for ideas on how to create your own writing sanctuary.

ACKNOWLEDGEMENTS

This book would not have been possible without the encouragement, guidance and support of a unique group of people.

To my mentors and lecturers at Regent's University, whose passion for their craft inspired me to get stuff written! Thanks to Diane Samuels, Ella Hickson, John Foster, Anna Jones, Ben Musgrave, David Hanson and Line Langebek. Special thanks to Phil Hughes, whose wit and wisdom are unparalleled.

To the writers, living and dead, who continue to inspire me. Notably Alecky Blythe, David Henry Hwang, Suzan-Lori Parks, Alan Bennett, Doug Wright, Edward Albee, Harold Pinter, Julia Davis, Sally Wainwright and Tina Fey. Most importantly, to Victoria Wood for an education in comedy, pathos, the human condition and how to explain it. As she said herself, '*One life per person is not enough. Not enough.*'

Thanks to my fellow scribes John White, Lindsey Jenkinson and Siân Rowland, who are always happy to read my work and encourage the next draft.

To the producers and artistic directors who have brought my work to stage and screen, thank you for the opportunities.

Finally, a huge thanks to Matt Applewhite at Nick Hern Books for making the dream of publishing this collection of writing exercises a reality, and to Nick Hern for inviting me to be part of the NHB family.

PART ONE

MINDFUL MEDITATION BEFORE WRITING

With the impulse to write, some writers can just sit down and write. They have the focus to hit the keys or spill some ink, and plant words on the page on demand. Perhaps you are one of those writers? For the rest of us, however, procrastination and writing often go hand in hand – we are the creators of magical new worlds, the makers of intriguing characters and weavers of wonderfully tangled plotlines… but sometimes, getting them out of our heads and onto the page can feel like a task best left for another day.

Whilst this book has been written as an aid to bypass any bumps in the road and to help overcome moments of writer's block, this first part is a little different. Here we will explore how mindful meditation can help you to get the most out of your writing time, by cleansing the mind of clutter. Implementing this practice as a precursor to a writing session will afford you clarity and focus – leaving any distractions outside of your writing space.

Mindful meditation is widely accepted to have plenty of health benefits; most relevant to our purpose are decreased stress levels, increased positivity and improved attention – all of which can set us up for a great writing session. I began attending a yin yoga class a few years ago and found the meditative 'surrender' style of the classes so profoundly relaxing that I wanted to introduce some of the elements into my daily writing practice.

Participants in my writing workshops have enjoyed indulging in mindful meditation exercises, and often remark how energised and inspired they feel afterwards – geared up for a productive day of writing! In response to this, I have created three five-minute meditation exercises for you to try.

Set the Scene

Your writing room, study or space is your sanctuary. Close the blinds or curtains, light a candle and play gentle relaxation music to create a calming atmosphere. I love using the ready-made meditation and yoga playlists on Spotify for this… panpipes, white noise, bird song, a babbling brook... whatever will help you to tune out.

Californian white sage is a sacred herb that has been used by Native Americans for thousands of years to purify the energy of an environment. It is also great for removing feelings of negativity and providing an immediate lift within a space. I recommend burning a sage 'smudge stick' for a minute or so to renew and restore the energy within your writing space each day.

Get Comfortable

Lie on the floor, on a yoga mat, a rug, or just on the carpet. Make sure you are comfortable enough to spend five minutes or longer here. If you are not able to get down to the ground, a comfortable chair, or even lying on a bed will work too. Rest your arms on the ground beside you, or if seated, place them on your lap; palms open.

Meditations

Once you have found your happy place, try one of the following meditations, each about five minutes long. You can find audio recordings of the meditations at the following website: www.nickhernbooks.co.uk/writers-toolkit-meditations

Begin by listening to the introductory Tune Out (track 1.0), followed by your choice of meditation. Lie back, hit play and relax to start your day. Alternatively, as you become more familiar with the recordings, you may wish to perform the meditation from memory, adding any variations or extensions to suit your needs.

Tune Out ▶1.0

Close your eyes. Focus on your breath. Note each inhalation over a mental count of five... Then exhale over a count of five... Counting will help you focus and clear your mind of the world outside of this space. Slow, even breaths. Before you know it, you will forget you are even counting.

Notice how your chest and belly expand... Allow your body to sink into the ground... and then... Relax. Each new breath is a moment in time carved out for you, a precious moment of deep relaxation, where no one can ask anything of you, and the world outside of your sanctuary demands nothing from you.

This is your sacred time. If your mind starts to wander from time to time, that's okay... Begin to count again and gently refocus.

Meet Your Muse

You're relaxing on a peaceful tropical island. The gentle sound of waves ripples along the shore. The sun spills down onto your body, gently flickering across your face. The warm sea breeze drifts across your arms and legs. You feel safe in this space.

After a moment... you notice a person in the distance. They walk slowly towards you, carrying a letter. You know this person. Perhaps they are a character from one of your previous works, or a new character you've yet to write about. You feel safe in their presence.

Very slowly, they move closer towards you... their eyes, mouth and spirit smiling all at once. Gently, they place the letter into your hands. As you look down towards the folded page, an immense feeling of excitement fills your body. Your eyes smile in appreciation as the person slowly leaves you in the tranquillity of your thoughts. Further and further they walk into the distance... back along the shore... until they have disappeared from sight.

Slowly, you open the letter. Go ahead... in your mind, read the first line to yourself. Now allow the words to play over and over in your mind. You hear them clearly. You see them sparkling vividly on the page. You know these words because they are yours. You wrote them.

Where the words live, who might speak them and what they might mean are an exciting stimulus to begin your writing session with.

In your own time, without rushing, slowly return to the room. Open your eyes, and when you feel ready to do so, sit up. If you have a whiteboard or noticeboard in your writing space, go ahead and write down those words now so that you can see them for the rest of the day. Otherwise, jot them down in a meditation notebook. One day, if not today, they might be the key to crashing through a writing roadblock.

Message in a Bottle ▶1.2

Imagine you are lying under a tree on a beautiful grassy riverbank. Sunlight dances across your closed eyelids as it peeps through the branches above you, which sway back and forth ever so gently in the breeze.

The sound of silence is only broken by the faint trickle of water from the river, as it ambles over smooth stones. Stay here a while. You are content. Nature has provided all that you require for this moment.

As your mind drifts in and out of a gentle slumber, you notice another sound in the distance. The soft twinkle of a glass wind chime, playing delicately in the breeze. With each deep inhale and exhale of your breath, you hear the chime sound. After a moment, looking down to the river, you see a small glass bottle with a long neck. The weight of its bottom allows it to sit upright in the water. Each time the wind sweeps past, it tilts gently from side to side. As it sweeps across the stones beneath, a chime rings out. Having connected the sound with the picture, you feel satisfied and relaxed. Enjoy this moment.

Feel the grass brushing against your feet as you step slowly down to the riverside. You notice how the sunlight reflects off the glass bottle as it drifts gradually towards you. Your eye is drawn to something inside of the bottle. Reaching your hand into the clear water, you pick up the bottle and take out a note from inside. As you unfold the paper, a single phrase is written inside.

Read the words aloud. Allow them to whirl around in your mind. What could they mean? Place the note back inside the bottle and step slowly back from the water's edge. As you lie back down under the tree, sunbeams shimmer across your eyes. In your own time, when it feels right to do so, open your eyes and return to the room. Make a note of the phrase from the bottle in your meditation notebook. It will serve you in the future.

MINDFUL MEDITATION

Today is Wonderful ▶1.3

With each breath you inhale, imagine a vibrant and brilliant white light entering your body. With each exhale, this light reaches a new part of your body, from your fingertips to your toes. The illumination is charged with positive energy. It makes you feel good about yourself and the work you will create today.

Feel it tingle through each fingertip with the words you will be empowered to write. Feel it nourish your creativity for the leaps you will take in progressing your current project. Feel it charge through your veins, giving you the strength to leap over any hurdles you might face today. Your entire body is alive with positive, creative energy, and the blank page awaits the words which only you can give.

Now use this energy to fill your sanctuary with positive words and vibes. Today is wonderful, and I am empowered to write. Go ahead… Repeat this aloud… *'Today is wonderful, and I am empowered to write.'* Take a deep breath and say it once more. *'Today is wonderful, and I am empowered to write.'* It feels good, right? Now, in your mind, repeat this line five more times, allowing the white light to enter and fill your body with each deep breath you take.

In your own time, start to wiggle your toes and fingers… then gently stretch your arms and legs. Now slowly open your eyes. Remember… Today *is* wonderful, and you are empowered to write!

A Final Stretch

Balasana, also known as child's pose, is a resting pose that stretches the hips, thighs and legs whilst calming the mind and relieving stress and tension. If you choose to do so, move into child's pose for a final stretch at the end of your meditation.

Start in a tabletop shape, on your hands and knees. Release the tops of your feet to the floor and bring your knees wider than your hips, big toes touching. Slowly lower your hips so that you are sitting on your heels. Now walk your hands forward and rest your head on the floor, or on a prop or rolled towel for support if required. Take several slow breaths into your belly and chest. To release, gently return to tabletop shape.

Experiment with these meditations and adapt them to suit your own needs, or try making up your own. Why not invent a new one each day? There are no rules, just go wherever your mind takes you and be open to experiencing whatever it is that your current writing project requires. Enjoy renewed focus and clarity without pressure or expectation.

Props	Benefits
Notebook and pen	Decreased stress
Background music	Increased positivity
White sage smudge stick or incense for burning	Improved attention
A yoga mat, rug or towel	Ideas for your writing

PART TWO

WARMING UP YOUR WRITING MUSCLE

Sometimes, if I'm feeling daunted by the prospect of tackling a problematic scene or simply don't feel inspired to work on my current project, then completing a short, unrelated writing exercise can be just the thing to help find my writing groove and refocus my mind.

Whilst Part 3 of this book offers exercises to help with the fundamental elements of playwriting, the activities in this section are generic, and can be used to warm up your writing muscle and simply to get your fingers typing – totally judgement-free and without expectation to deliver anything of note. The results are for your eyes only, so you can try the exercises again and again, with totally different results every time.

Starting your day with a short exercise can be a great way to jump-start your writing session. What better way to take on a demanding work in progress, than with a sense of achievement and boost of confidence, having already completed a quick assignment.

The following exercises can all be completed in roughly ten to fifteen minutes. But don't worry… if you don't have time for that, simply skip ahead to Part 7 and pick one of the speedy, two-minute writing prompts to begin your day.

Freewriting/Freetalking

'Start writing, no matter what.
The water does not flow until the faucet is turned on.'

Louis L'Amour

*If mindful meditation (in Part 1 of this book) serves as a
Ctrl+Alt+Del for your conscious mind, then freewriting
continues with the blank page you find yourself looking at. I think
of freewriting as less of a writing exercise and more of a physical
warm-up for me as a writer. In much the same way that a singer
needs to warm up their vocal cords before a concert, it is good
practice for writers to warm our writing muscle and re-engage
and reconnect with our creativity before launching into or
continuing a piece of work.*

Freewriting

Many writers will be familiar with the practice of freewriting,
but here I'm going to offer an expansion on this classic. I have
included this exercise so that this book may serve as a
comprehensive resource tool for writers at all stages.

The main aim of freewriting is to write continuously for a set
period – I recommend five to ten minutes if your schedule
permits. Sit comfortably at your desk and just allow your hand
to write (no computers allowed here). Now just keep writing,
anything that comes into your head. Don't worry about
grammar, punctuation, spelling… just write. It doesn't need to
look neat and doesn't even need to make sense or be legible,
the purpose is simply to empty a continuous stream of words
from your mind onto the page. The most important thing
here is to keep writing. If you find yourself lost for words at
any point, simply write *'I am writing I am writing I am writing I
am writing'*, until something new comes to mind.

This is freewriting in a nutshell. You can pick a single random word to inspire a flood of thoughts, or use something related to whatever it is that you are working on.

If you are currently working on a scene or section of dialogue from a project, freewrite about this. Picture the scene in your mind's eye and tune into the conversation between the characters in it – allow your hand to write away as you listen. As you hear the 'live' voices of your characters whirling around your mind, permit them to overlap, cut each other short, sharing fragments of thoughts and feelings, heartache or joy – in this way, perhaps soundbites and clues that you might have missed within the confines of the scene will be captured on the page. If we remember that all our characters have a life beyond the tiny windows through which we see them in our work, there are an abundance of experiences and feelings that we only really scratch the surface of. Freewriting is a great way to hear from your characters, beyond the world of the play.

Perhaps you still won't find your way into the scene, but you may just learn something crucial about one of your characters, which in turn might inform or unlock something elsewhere in their story, which may help you progress with another scene. What do they really want? What makes them tick... or ticks them off? What are they most passionate about? What do they think about the other characters in the story? Can you decode their thoughts captured from your own stream of consciousness?

For more information on this practice, consider reading *The Artist's Way* by Julia Cameron (Tarcher/Putnam, 1992), who encourages filling three pages with freewriting every single morning, in what she calls 'morning pages'.

Freetalking

As an extension of freewriting, freetalking is something that I often do with writers in my workshops and classes, creating an orchestra of overlapping voices similar to someone turning a radio dial and skipping across multiple frequencies. I have found that it is equally effective in a solo writing environment… why not give it a try?

Once you are in the freewriting groove and you hear your characters talking freely on the page, you may find that your hand is unable to keep up with the speed at which the voices are speaking to you. That's okay! Let their voices out! As characters begin to overlap in your mind, start to speak one (or more) voice aloud and write the others. If it helps, try playing some gentle classical music in the background. It might feel a little uncomfortable hearing your own voice at first but you'll soon relax into it.

Alternatively, stop writing at this point, close your eyes and speak both voices, one after the other in a semi-conscious free-flowing dialogue. In the safety of your writing space, give yourself total freedom to talk in tongues and wander off on a tangent, almost in an act of spiritualism or clairvoyance. There is no right and wrong way to approach this, the purpose is simply to play and experiment. I don't suggest recording your freetalking sessions, as doing so may add pressure to extract something usable from the exercise, which misses the point. Instead, simply allow the voices to flow in a stream of consciousness. In my experience, any worthy nuggets of information, scene ideas or specific words I hear my characters speaking will remain imprinted in the front of my mind at the end of the session, inspiring me to commit them to paper soon after.

Pygmalion's Seagull

Almost everybody will at some point in their life have played Consequences – an old parlour game in which players take it in turns to add a line to a story on a piece of paper, before folding it over and passing it along to the next player. Once everyone has added to the story, it is read aloud, often with hilarious results.

Whilst this is a fun warm-up exercise for a writing group, done alone it's rather like playing a game of chess by yourself! So here is my take on this classic, reinvented for the solo writer…

Pick two playscripts by different authors from your bookshelf. Open the first script at any page and choose a character from that page. Write down their name and their first line of dialogue from that page. Now pick up your second script and do the same. Continue in this manner, switching between texts and stopping at a new page each time; finding the same character on that page and selecting their first line of dialogue. Write as much or as little as you like, sometimes the shortest exchanges can be the funniest.

You can repeat this exercise again and again, with totally different results every time. You might even try this with three scripts. If you ever wondered what would happen if Dotty Otley from *Noises Off* crossed paths with Meg Boles from *The Birthday Party*… or if Eliza Doolittle met King Lear… *now is your chance to find out!*

This exercise can also provide a little light relief at the end of a writing session when working on a challenging or emotional piece of writing.

Zooconomy

From the sublime to the ridiculous... This exercise encourages you to let go of reality and have fun with creative writing. I enjoy this kind of warm-up equally before working on a comedic piece, or as a little light relief when working on a serious one.

Open your internet browser and navigate to your 'go-to' news source. Search for a potentially dull economic/business story... perhaps the Chancellor of the Exchequer's latest budget announcement or a troubled trade agreement.

Now let's have some fun! First, copy and paste the article into a new text document, so that you can edit the story. Next, decide on a theme. For the purpose of this example, I'm going to use animals at the zoo, but you might also use aliens in a far-away galaxy, toddlers in a kindergarten, or even the bizarre acts in a travelling circus. Go through the story and switch things up...

- Wherever you see a name, change it to an animal.

- Wherever you see a place, change it to an area in the zoo.

- Wherever you see a commodity, change it to a food.

- Wherever you see a quote, change it to a fitting literary quote.

You can change whatever you like – just decide on the rules at the beginning and have fun rewriting the story. Here's an example...

> *The President of the Lion Enclosure says he is ready to intensify his trade war with Primates by slapping tariffs on all banana imports from the Monkey House. 'I am as vigilant as a cat to steal cream,' he said in an interview with the ZOO Channel. The big cat's comments come before the most recent round of Lion tariffs has had time*

to take effect. Last week, the enclosure listed £250bn worth of additional Monkey products on which it intends to impose tariffs as soon as the rainy season ends. The list named more than six thousand items including figs, rodents, rope bridges, and tyre swings, to be subject to a 10% tariff.

This exercise is very simple, yet a really creative way to jump into a writing session. It's so quick, you could pick a dull news story every morning and 'funny it up' to get your creative juices flowing.

Scene-Bombing

We're all familiar with photo-bombing – the act of inserting yourself into someone else's photo. But what about scene-bombing? Try this as a fun, warm-up idea.

Take a favourite character from one of your own plays or screenplays, and allow their world to collide with that of a well-known movie or play.

In the example below, I have replaced the character of Mrs Cheveley from Oscar Wilde's *An Ideal Husband* (1895) with a Lancashire tea lady, Valerie Macintosh, from my 2005 comedy cabaret *Tickled Pink!* In the example below, taken from Act Three of Wilde's play, Lord Goring finds Valerie snooping in his drawing room...

> LORD GORING *rushes to the door of the drawing-room, when* ~~MRS CHEVELEY~~ VALERIE *comes out, looking* ~~radiant and much amused~~ *flustered and guilty*.
>
> VALERIE (*bowing and curtseying profusely*). Evenin' sir, Lord Goring, sir!
>
> LORD GORING. Mrs. Macintosh! Great heavens!... May I ask what you were doing in my drawing room?
>
> VALERIE. Baltic tonight, sir! Thought I'd...err... chuck another log on t' fire! Just in case, like. Tek chill off, so to speak!
>
> LORD GORING. Doesn't that sound rather like tempting Providence?
>
> VALERIE. Well, that's as maybe. (*Pause.*) Happen I'll fire up t' urn and mek thee a brew before I shoot off, eh? (*She goes to leave.*)
>
> LORD GORING. I am glad you have called. I am going to give you some good advice.

VALERIE (*stopping*). With all due what-nots, sir…
there's nowt thee can teach me about mekin' a brew.
I'm third-generation tea lady. It's in me blood. Prick
me, sir. I'll bleed Lapsang all the day long!

LORD GORING. I see you are quite as wilful as you
used to be.

VALERIE. That I am, sir. Now, you wait here, I'll see if
I can't find thee a spare Eccles cake in t' pantry.
(*Muttering.*) Good advice! (*She goes to leave again.*)

LORD GORING. Too much experience is a dangerous
thing. Pray, have a cigarette. Half the pretty women
in London smoke cigarettes. Personally I prefer the
other half.

VALERIE. Give over, Lord Goring, sir… wharra ya
like?! I've not had a fag since God were a lad.

LORD GORING. You have come here to sell me
Robert Chiltern's letter, haven't you?

VALERIE (*confused*). Bobby Chiltern? Does he play
for Wigan? (*She notices him eyeing up a small
booklet in the front of her pinny.*) Oh! Your Avon
order! Why didn't you say, sir?

LORD GORING. Because you haven't mentioned the
subject. Have you got it with you?

VALERIE (*sitting down*). Now… I couldn't get that
foaming moisturiser yer wanted, sir, but I've an
illuminating gel 'ere that'll reinforce the skin's
natural protective moisture barrier and have yer
lookin' babby smooth by Tuesday. Cherie Blair
swears by it. (*Beat.*) Shall I pop thee down for two?

LORD GORING. What is your price for it?

VALERIE. Hundred mill for six quid… or a twin-pack
for a tenner. (*He hands her the cash – she refuses.*)

LORD GORING. What do you want then, Mrs Macintosh?

VALERIE. Please, call me Val.

LORD GORING *tenses as* VALERIE *starts to remove her pinny and edges towards him.*

Go for it... allow extreme worlds to collide! Write your Mr Darcy character into *Trainspotting*, or your sceptical detective into *The Truman Show*. You will find plenty of classic playscripts in the public domain, and thousands of screenplays available to read online for free. Check out the following websites:

- www.openlibrary.org
- www.simplyscripts.com
- www.imsdb.com
- www.weeklyscript.com
- www.sfy.ru
- www.gutenberg.org

Crosswords

This exercise is simple, quick and a lot of fun… in fact, you can do it on the bus, on the subway or in a café whilst you have your breakfast. It's a great instant-writing exercise for those who love sipping coffee and people-watching… under the guise of tackling the morning crossword!

Pick up a copy of today's newspaper and start by having a go at completing the crossword. Or, if you don't have the time or inclination, just look at the answers to yesterday's puzzle. Looking around you, select two people random, they might be sat opposite you in the café or on the bus. Let's name one of them Across, and the other Down.

Your challenge is to write a scene between Across and Down, including their respective crossword answers, in number order, into their dialogue. Here is an example, based on two soldiers who were sipping coffee opposite me as I wrote this…

ACROSS
1. Thought to be guilty (7) [*Answer: Suspect*]
6. Gambling city (4) [*Answer: Reno*]

DOWN
1. Gesture or action (6) [*Answer: Signal*]
2. Became more profound (8) [*Answer: Deepened*]

Then you might start your dialogue like this:

ACROSS. The *suspect* is in view, stand by to move in.

DOWN. System locked and loaded, sir. Awaiting command *signal*.

ACROSS. Wait! Before you do this, just know… that night in *Reno*…

DOWN. I know. Our love, it… *deepened,* right? I felt it
too, sir. (*Pause.*) Sir?

Start by writing alternating character names, Across and
Down, down the left margin of your page. Do this ten or so
times for each, leaving only a single line of your page for each
line of dialogue which will help to keep things snappy. It
doesn't even matter if your answers to the crossword are
incorrect, just pick an alternative word that fits the space
available. Have fun with it and go wherever the random
words take you.

One Step Forward

It was the playwright Ella Hickson who first simplified storytelling for me during a lecture at Regent's University, where I was studying for my master's degree. Stripping away the fear of dramatic structure, Ella cut through the theory and boiled storytelling down to this: 'Plays simply follow a character through time in pursuit of a desire.' *Humans like to overcomplicate things, and writers can tend to overthink things… so considering the simplicity of this principle certainly makes the task of penning a masterpiece, or just getting to the end of a first draft, seem a little less daunting.*

'Great,' *I thought.* 'Let's do it! How hard can that be?' *Ella then upended said character's desire (their intention) with a conflict (obstacle), reminding the class that* 'Without conflict, there is no drama.' *A conflicting force must be at play in order to make, say, a character's trip to the library to return a book (intention) a little less straightforward (obstacle).*

Still, when you approach writing with such simplicity in mind, writing a great story needn't be so hard. Let's try it out.

Keeping things simple, write down a new character name and identify a single desire – e.g. *Bernard. Wants to grab a coffee on his way to work.* Next, in prose, write a simple starting point for your character's journey – e.g. *Petting his cat goodbye, Bernard closes the door to his townhouse and throws his scarf over his shoulder as he sets off for his local coffee shop.* We are going to let fate decide what happens next. How dramatic can we make Bernard's simple quest for a flat white when we add conflict to the mix? Go ahead and flip a coin and find out.

- *Heads*: Your character takes one step towards their desire.
- *Tails*: An obstacle sets your character one step back in their pursuit.

At this point, it's worth remembering that conflict comes in two forms: internal and external. The two are not mutually exclusive and can play out simultaneously. Internal conflict is defined as a struggle that takes place within a character, usually around a question of conscience, a choice they must make, or the action they decide to take next. With external conflict, we are talking about antagonistic forces outside of the character's control. In both cases, conflict is simply the 'obstacles' to the characters 'intentions', which make our stories compelling. Without conflict, Bernard's trip to the coffee shop would be a pretty dull story.

There are usually three main subtypes of external conflict.

- *Character vs Character*: A character struggles against another. Think 'hero vs villain'. This type of conflict is usually motivated by survival, greed, power, love, morality or duty. Sometimes each character has a different goal, and they stand in each other's way. Other times, they might both want the same thing and must fight to get it.

- *Character vs Society*: Think 'one vs many', with someone or a group of people going against the grain, or against wider society to fight for something. Examples include the coal miners in *Billy Elliot*, striking to protest colliery closures by the National Coal Board. Or Billy Elliot himself, battling small-minded stereotypes about boys doing ballet.

- *Character vs Nature*: Battles against nature and the elements are a staple of the fantasy, thriller and adventure genres. Think sharks, dragons, snakes, hurricanes, tornados, volcanoes and earthquakes. Characters confronted by acts of god, wild beasts or hostile environments.

Some examples of internal and external conflict as they relate to Bernard's story might include:

- Internal conflict:

  - Should he spend money on coffee when he can make a cup at home?

  - Can he be sure the coffee he's drinking has been ethically sourced?

  - His cat will be lonely… maybe he should stay at home?

- External conflict:

  - There is a bus strike so he will have to walk, slowing him down and making him late for his next appointment.

  - He is mugged on his way, and the thief steals his wallet. Now he can't buy a coffee and probably can't make it to his appointment.

  - A freak thunderstorm forces him to take shelter somewhere, throwing him off course and possibly causing the coffee shop to close too.

Flip a coin several times. Remember, 'heads' puts your character on an upward trajectory, takings steps towards their desire. 'Tails' puts an unexcepted obstacle in their path, making an otherwise simple want or desire tougher for your character to achieve. Their journey and your story will be all the more dramatic for it.

See *Exercise 3.1.12: Daddy or Chips?* on page 61 for another exercise exploring internal conflict.

The Inspirator

Waiting for inspiration to strike? Stop waiting and start writing!

Pick two character names from the list below and write them
at the top of your page. Decide on an age for each of the
characters and write this next to their name. Now choose one
occupation, like, dislike and character trait for each of the
characters and write these under each of their names. Finally,
select a location and an opening line of dialogue. Use as much
of the character information as you can to write a spontaneous
duologue between the two characters you have created.

Names

Rory	Sky	Scarlett
Dave	Samantha	Eddie
Angel	Alex	Oakley
Stan	Lennon	Penelope
Dakota	Blue	Sue
Bruce	Michael	Maggie
Dennis	Morgan	Vic
Storm	North	Frank
Brendan	Phoenix	Devon

Occupation

Decorated Navy Seal	Window fitter	Call-centre operator
Landscape painter	Circus clown	Coastguard
Writer	College student	Meteorologist
Ostrich farmer	Medical receptionist	Midwife
Social worker	Entrepreneur	Firefighter
Church volunteer	Gas-station attendant	Psychic
CCTV operator	Gardener	Senior marketing exec
Dentist	Pro-wrestler	Librarian
Full-time parent		

Likes or dislikes

Bacon	Confrontation	Romance
Vegan cheese	Cats	Family time
Right-wing politics	Energy drinks	Horoscopes
Thrifty living	Camping	Knitting
Being single	Video games	The dark
Political correctness	Celery	Exercise
Fine wines	Travel	Winter
Green tea	Sudoku	People
	Rap music	Marmite

Character trait

Adventurous	Fun-loving	Popular
Ambitious	Funny	Pretty
Bossy	Gentle	Prim
Brave	Generous	Proper
Bright	Happy	Proud
Cheerful	Hard-working	Quiet
Compassionate	Helpful	Reserved
Conceited	Honest	Responsible
Considerate	Humble	Sad
Cooperative	Imaginative	Self-confident
Courageous	Impulsive	Selfish
Creative	Independent	Serious
Curious	Intelligent	Shy
Daring	Inventive	Smart
Dark	Joyful	Strong
Demanding	Keen	Studious
Disagreeable	Lazy	Successful
Dreamer	Lovable	Thoughtful
Energetic	Loyal	Timid
Excited	Messy	Tireless
Fancy	Mischievous	Wild
Fighter	Neat	Witty
Friendly	Patriotic	Zealous

Locations

Maternity ward	Death row	Amish barn raising
Route 66 gas station	Hell	Airport security
	A Greek restaurant	Police car
Backstage at the opera	North Korean jail	Stalled subway train
	Starbucks on Mars	
Nuclear-war bunker	Hotel wedding breakfast	American Embassy Awards ceremony

Opening lines

- You should have never let her inside the apartment.

- It's not what you think.

- Don't you dare come any closer!

- It was the only way to silence him!

- That's not what I meant!

- It was only supposed to keep her still for a minute!

- I didn't know he couldn't swim!

- Check the label, you must have got the dosage wrong!

- My other hat is a sombrero.

- Is that your mother's dress?

- Have you washed your hands?

- They're coming. Close your eyes.

PART THREE

THE ELEMENTS

This part of the book features exercises for each of the following elements of writing for stage and screen:

- Character
- Dialogue
- Subtext
- Setting
- Plot

The focus here is on the practical process of writing. So, if you need help creating or developing characters, writing naturalistic or stylised dialogue, adding depth to a scene with subtext, defining a sense of place or thinking about new ways to advance your plot, then turn to the relevant part of the book and try out an exercise to set you on the right track.

Likewise, if you find yourself staring at your computer screen, or procrastination or distraction are starting to take over, decide which area you are unable to move past and try using one of these exercises to fine-tune your work or leapfrog that hurdle.

CHARACTER

'I find my characters and stories in many varied places; sometimes they pop out of newspaper articles, obscure historical texts, lively dinner-party conversations and some even crawl out of the dusty remote recesses of my imagination.'

Lynn Nottage

All great scripts need great characters. They must be believable, have depth and a convincing arc, which makes the audience want to go on a journey with them. To meet these criteria and create wonderfully intriguing and complex characters, we need to understand the characters' backstories and what makes them who they are. The exercises in this part of the book are designed to help you create, explore, define and interrogate your characters and their function within your scripts.

Getting to Know You

Writing a character profile is a quick way to throw a lot of background information onto the page and start to get a sense of the characters who will inhabit your world, be they human, animal or machine. Of course, you will list a whole host of information which will never end up in your script, and that is precisely as it should be. Understanding everything that makes up your characters will help you build a holistic, fully formed picture of characters that are believable, yet beautifully flawed.

Let's start with the basics. Go ahead and list the following in your notebook:

- Name

- Age

- Place of birth

- Nationality

- Education and occupation

- Distinguishing physical features

Now let's look at the way your character presents:

- Are they confident, shy, powerful, dominating or insecure?

- Is their speech fast, slow, a drawl, impaired or measured?

- Do they sound well educated? Do they have an accent or use slang?

- How do they carry themselves (e.g. relaxed, stiff, military or slouched)?

Just like you and me, characters are a product of their environment. Next, let's think about how a character's background and life experiences have shaped who they are today:

- Who are their immediate family?

- Briefly describe their childhood (e.g. happy, sad, neglected, spoilt, in care, etc.).

- What are their best and worst childhood memories?

- As a child, what was/is their dream for the future?

- What advice would they give to their younger self?

- Who were/are their closest childhood friends? Describe their relationship.

- Did they, or do they have any enemies? If so, why?

Looking at your character today, how would they reflect on the following:

- Their biggest regret?

- Their biggest flaw?

- Their greatest strength?

- Their biggest fear?

- Their greatest accomplishment?

- Their most embarrassing moment?

- Do they have any secrets or skeletons in their closet?

Briefly describe how your character would react in the following scenarios:

- A stressful situation, like being asked to step aside at airport security.

- A blind date with someone they are not attracted to.

- Being promoted at work over a close friend who was in line for the job.

- Being overlooked for career promotion in favour of a close friend.

CHARACTER

- The death of a close friend or family member.

- Winning the lottery.

- Discovering that they have a terminal illness.

Looking forward to the future, think about:

- What do they want the most in the whole world?

- What are the top five things on your character's bucket list?

- Where do they see themselves in five, ten and twenty years' time?

Thinking now about the world of the play or screenplay, and the window in time in which we meet your character: what is their raison d'être? Try to answer the following point in a single paragraph:

- What is their central objective?

- What is their driving force or motivation for this?

Your answers to these final two questions will provide a blueprint for your character's journey, which you can use to realign your focus and stay on track whilst writing. I find it helpful to write these two points, along with the answers for each character, on index cards and pin them to my story wall (see page 161) when working on a project.

By now you should have a fully formed picture of your character and know a little more about their likes, dislikes, wants, regrets and the environments which have made them who they are today. Test this new knowledge by writing a letter as your current character, to their older or younger self. Doing so in the form of an apology, a plea or a request will likely validate the answers you have just identified in the final two questions in this section.

The Willard Project

This exercise has become a staple character-creation exercise in my writing workshops because it is both immersive and thought-provoking. The source material is rich, whilst the brief is wide-open for the writer to imagine and create. It is fascinating to observe the vastly different interpretations of the same source material when given to different writers.

'In 1995, when the Willard Psychiatric Center in Willard, New York, was closed, staff members surveyed the contents of the buildings and they discovered an attic containing over four hundred patient suitcases. The cases dated from between 1910 and the late 1960s and were saved by Willard employees after the deaths of the patients. Many of them appeared untouched since their owners packed them decades earlier before entering the institution. The suitcases and their contents bear witness to the rich, complex lives their owners lived prior to being committed to Willard. They speak about aspirations, accomplishments, community connections, but also about loss and isolation.'

www.suitcaseexhibit.org

Photographs of the Willard Suitcases Collection © 2020 Jon Crispin (www.willardsuitcases.com).

Choose one of the cases and study the photograph. Looking at the personal artefacts in the case, think about who its owner might have been and the life they might have led before they disappeared behind hospital walls. Now write a quick character profile for this person based on the contents of their case. Here are some things to consider:

- What were the owner's career, hobbies or interests?

- Who were their family and friends? Who have they left behind?

- What were their hopes and dreams as a young child? Were they realised?

- What is the one thing they longed for?

- Why was this person committed to Willard?

In many of the photographs, we can see clues about the owners' happy memories. However, there are also suggestions of lives coming apart, unemployment, poverty, the loss of loved ones and loneliness. It's amazing what you can glean from what people pack in a suitcase, what a person holds near and dear, and the clues such possessions might reveal about their personality.

Now that you have a picture of the life of the owner in your mind and have written a short character profile, rewind to the day that they arrived at the institution. Imagine them entering and the door to the outside world closing behind them. The only connection to their former life is the suitcase they hold and its contents. Now write the first letter that this person might send to a friend, relative, doctor or other acquaintance on the outside world. I suggest writing with paper and a pencil for a deeper connection to the scenario. Here are some things to think about:

- Would they feel anger towards the person or events which lead to them being institutionalised?

- Would they worry about a loved one, child or elderly relative left behind?

- Would they be positive about a speedy recovery and share plans for their future?

- Would they despair and have little to hope or live for?

Check out the book for more information, *The Lives They Left Behind: Suitcases from a State Hospital Attic* by Darby Penney and Peter Stastny (Bellevue Literary Press, 2008).

Remember Me?

We all have friends with whom we have lost touch. Think back to all the people you went through school with as a child; the kids you went to after-school clubs with, or saw at swimming classes or violin lessons each week. Perhaps you may only remember faces and can't recall their names. Or maybe a name has stuck in your head after all these years, but you have lost the clarity of their appearance. Do you ever wonder if they still remember you?

Pick a character from one of your plays or screenplays – someone whose backstory has yet to be fully established, and whom you would like to know a little more about. Let's assume that merely out of curiosity your character has looked up an old school friend (or foe) online and they decide to reach out.

From the perspective of your character, think about the things that they might say and the questions that they might ask. Now write the message that your character would send to their long-lost acquaintance.

Here are some pointers:

- Reintroduce yourself. Did you have a memorable nickname? Have you changed your name since school?

- Give assurance. Is there a shared memory that will aid the recipient's memory of you? Maybe you had a crush on the same person, or you wore a distinctive hat? Maybe you famously wet yourself at the Christmas carol concert?

- Bring your story up to date. What have you been doing since school? Did your life/career take you in an unexpected direction? Have you left your home town?

- So much to catch up on! Ask about their life since school – kids/marriage/career?

- Shared connections. Do you keep in touch with anyone from your old social circle, or perhaps you want to ask if they do? You might even have a recent story or anecdote about a former classmate you would like to share.

- Questions? Is there anything about your home town, old school friends, past teachers or crushes that this person might be able to update you on?

Asking questions of an old friend in this way will no doubt get you thinking about the background of your character and how their formative years shaped the person they are today.

Imagine you have hit 'send' on your message. Now you must play the waiting game. No doubt you are now thinking of even more questions that you wish you had asked. If so, jot them down in a notebook for a follow-up message.

After a day or so, open your original message and read it from the point of view of the recipient. Remember the sender (your character) as a young person and attempt to reply to their message. Doing so will provide a credible backstory for your character and allow you to know them in a way you may not have before. For example, perhaps you can gain a greater sense of understanding, informed by a traumatic experience in their childhood? For instance, if the recipient recalls a peer whom they remember was mean to your character, then you might use this to relate your character's fear of confrontation, or trace their insecurities back to playground bullying.

The insight you can glean from an exercise like this can be invaluable to informing your work and building characters who are relatable and fully fleshed out. Try this exercise for other characters in your work.

THE ELEMENTS

Stepping Stones

I'm a massive fan of Richard Harris's Stepping Out, *in all of its incarnations – the original 1984 play, the 1991 movie adaptation starring Liza Minnelli, and in 1996, the underrated musical version with lyrics by Mary Stewart-David and music by Denis King. Whichever version you read or watch,* Stepping Out *is a great lesson in character progression.*

The story unites eight people from diverse backgrounds through a weekly tap-dancing class. Their lives outside of the church hall spill over into rehearsals, and their differing motivations for attending the class are revealed... Andi is escaping an abusive husband, the bossy Vera is wealthy but bored and seeks friends, Rose is at her wit's end as the parent of a delinquent teenage son. Their instructor, Mavis (once an aspiring professional dancer, now trying to make ends meet) has entered them into a dance competition, which serves to unite the characters and provide a central plotline, whilst their individual journeys of self-discovery weave together to form a beautifully layered story.

For each character in your script, create a four-step growth chart. You will use this to identify critical steps on their individual journey: from initial conflict, followed by growth, through to their goals (whether or not they are achieved), and ultimately their change. Remember, every character needs to go on a journey, however big or small, and should be changed in some way by the end of the story. If not, this should lead you to question their purpose in your script. Here's an example based on the character of Andi (spoiler alert!).

CONFLICT

- Trapped in a loveless, abusive relationship.
- No self-confidence.
- No freedom – controlled by husband.

GROWTH

- Finds something for herself one night a week (dancing).
- Meets fellow tapper, Geoffrey, and feels a spark.
- Sees potential for happiness beyond her marriage.

GOAL

- Freedom.
- Happiness.
- Self-love and respect.
- Open to new possibilities.

CHANGE

- Realises she's pretty good at something (dancing).
- Confronts her husband.
- Open to being appreciated (and loved) – she agrees to have dinner with Geoffrey.

Start by drawing an empty growth chart like the one on the previous page, including the headings: conflict, growth, goal and change. Next, try to find three or four bullet points for each step for all of your characters.

Once you have completed some bullet-point information, notice how each step informs the next, whilst resolving the last, ultimately building towards a character change, rounding and concluding their journey.

Well-crafted secondary character subplots can be transformative for your primary characters whilst enhancing the main plot with additional conflict, comedy, triumph and pathos. This exercise should help you to realise the full story potential in each of your characters.

All Change, Please

'Sometimes a person has to go a very long distance out of his way to come back a short distance correctly.'

Edward Albee

As a species, it seems humans are programmed to resist change. Change interferes with autonomy and can often make people feel powerless, almost as if they have lost control. As writers, this presents us with a challenge each time we create a character. For our characters to go on successful journeys, emotionally or otherwise, they must be the subject of change, being altered or affected in one way or another. This might be in the form of realisation, or of an understanding of something they did not know in the beginning. Perhaps in gaining, winning or achieving whatever it is they set out to. Or maybe an event or circumstance has had a significant effect on them. Changes can be small or large, mind-changing or life-altering, but change must have been effected for a character's story arc to be fulfilling and/or satisfying, for them and for the audience.

One way to effect change is by understanding our character's limits. We can do this by thinking about what would need to happen in their world in order for them to be pushed beyond their comfort zone and towards an event or experience that will, in turn, result in a believable change, be it mentally, emotionally, physically, environmentally or otherwise. Thinking in this way will also highlight additional plot ideas and character potential.

Pick a character from either a project that you are currently writing or from a previous piece of work. Now draw a mind map with your character's name at the centre and begin to imagine around this, listing possible events, circumstances or situations which would be counterintuitive, highly unusual and totally out of character. For the purpose of this exercise, I suggest thinking bigger, or perhaps more extreme than might seem natural for the character and their story world – you can always exercise a lighter touch when using the learnt information to inform your character's choices within your script. For example...

- Jeremy Dale (a heartless and unscrupulous business owner)

  ○ Shares unexpected profits with employees by way of a surprise bonus.

  ○ Donates profits to an animal shelter.

  ○ Offers a struggling single parent an interest-free loan and paid leave.

- Kay Giddings (a caring and diligent adoption social worker)

  ○ Turns a blind eye to an unsafe environment during a home visit.

  ○ Abducts a sibling group and drives them across the country.

  ○ Steals cash from the purse of an adoptive parent during a home visit.

Using pens of two different colours, write a single word beside each of your ideas, to answer the following questions:

1. What would have to be at stake to force your character to make such a decision that would involve a fundamental character shift?

   ○ Life, death, love, health, money, peace, etc.

2. What is the resulting change for the character?

   ○ Mental, emotional, physical, environmental, etc.

Once you have completed this exercise, return to the reality of your script as it stands and reflect upon your character's story arc. What have they learned, experienced or felt by the final scene? Have they experienced a satisfying change that feels believable and honest to them, and to the broader story? If you are struggling to define this, review the mind map you have just created in this exercise and see if there is an idea you might be able to take forward and introduce within your script.

Remember, the lengths that your character is willing to go to, in order to achieve their want or desire, is what makes them and their story appealing to an audience. If the audience cares about them, or are moved to feel something for them along the way (favourably or unfavourably), then you have created a compelling character!

Cuddly Toy

'…Dinner service… fondue set… cuddly toy!' For anyone growing up in the UK from the early 1970s onwards, Saturday-night television meant one thing: The Generation Game. *The finale of the gameshow saw one member of the winning family watch prizes pass by on a conveyor belt, before trying to recall as many as possible in sixty seconds. Good times! Whilst a different assortment of prize items featured on the conveyor belt on* The Generation Game *each week, the one prize that always got a cheer from the studio audience was the cuddly toy.*

Objects or possessions can represent specific attitudes, feelings or actions for people. What items does your character hold dear? Set a timer for sixty seconds and try to list as many things as you can that mean something to your character.

Looking at your list, reflect on which objects might communicate the following meaning for your character. Can you highlight any objects which represent:

- A link to their past?

- Who they are as a person?

- A secret that they would not want anyone else to know about?

- Sentimentality/a softer side?

- A memory of a special person or place?

- The one item they would save if escaping a fire?

Count how many objects from your list already feature in your script, either physically or in reference. Now note how many mentions, glances, uses or comments each one of them earns. Does their meaning or relevance change throughout the story? When characters talk with each other, they are usually influenced by three different factors: their current mood/feelings, their expectations of the other characters in the scene or what they want from them and lastly, how they feel deep down about the other characters. However, a character's relationship to, possession or use of an inanimate object can be revealing of their genuine emotions without subtext or 'scene baggage'.

Fractured Fairy Tales

An archetype can be a challenge, symbol, idea, setting or a character which reflects the human condition. We'll look at the latter for the purpose of this exercise. Swiss psychologist Carl Jung maintained that the root of an archetype is in the 'collective unconscious' of mankind. Archetypes in fiction allow the reader or audience to make a connection between parts of themselves and parts of the characters. By including these in your writing, you can help your audience become more immersed and personally invested in the story through their connection to it.

The most apparent archetypes appear in fairy tales, most usually in the shape of heroes and villains, who often share the same characteristics from one story to the next, which is precisely what defines them as an archetype – to all intents, they serve the same primary function in any story.

Choose some common archetype characters from the list of Disney animated films below and write an original real-world scene in which they meet. If we forget for a second that Cinderella is the daughter of an aristocrat and that her hero is a prince, the fundamental character functions hold up and can be dressed up, transplanted to different worlds and serve the same purpose with significant effect – *a wealthy businessman falls in love with a down-on-her-luck Hollywood sex worker…* sound familiar? Using their well-known fairy-tale personas, think about the function that each of these character types will provide within your story.

- *The Innocent*: Open to adventure and new experiences. Truthful and honest.
    - Cinderella
    - Princess Jasmine (*Aladdin*)

- *The Hero*: Strong, courageous and faithful against all odds.
    - Prince Charming (*Cinderella*)

- ○ Aladdin
- ○ Simba (*The Lion King*)

- *The Sage*: Wise and decisive with clarity of thought at all times. A source of guidance for the Hero or the Innocent.
  - ○ Fairy Godmother (*Cinderella*)
  - ○ The Genie (*Aladdin*)
  - ○ Rafiki (*The Lion King*)

- *The Villain*: Cunning, deceptive and antagonistic. Plotting against the Innocent.
  - ○ Wicked Stepmother (*Cinderella*)
  - ○ Jafar (*Aladdin*)
  - ○ Scar (*The Lion King*)

- *The Accomplice*: Working for the Villain, often without morals or self-respect.
  - ○ The stepsisters (*Cinderella*)
  - ○ Iago (*Aladdin*)
  - ○ The hyenas (*The Lion King*)

- *The Jester*: Funny, eccentric and irreverent, often a confidant to the Hero or the Innocent.
  - ○ Jaq and Gus, the mice (*Cinderella*)
  - ○ Abu the monkey (*Aladdin*)
  - ○ Timon and Pumbaa (*The Lion King*)

- *The Sovereign*: Providing order, stability and keeping up traditions. Often offers a blessing or reward to the Hero.
  - ○ The King (*Cinderella*)
  - ○ The Sultan (*Aladdin*)
  - ○ Mufasa (*The Lion King*)

Have fun exploring how archetypes and their tried-and-tested functions can enhance your character creation.

THE ELEMENTS

But Why?

Interrogating your characters is a quick way to dig a little deeper and get to the bottom of things. Putting them on the spot and applying a little pressure can expose their true rationale and help you to understand their motivation in a scene.

Try this exercise if you're struggling to identify or clarify a character's motivation whilst writing a scene. You don't even need to write anything down here, just ask your character a simple question, and then respond to every answer they give with 'Why?' Here's an example:

> It's a party… why aren't you drinking?
> *I had a rough night last night.*
> Why?
> *It was Amanda's twenty-first, I probably drank too much and stayed out too late.*
> Why?
> *I wanted to be there until the end.*
> Why?
> *Because I wanted to make sure she got home okay.*
> Why?
> *I guess I have feelings for her.*
> Why?
> *I was hoping she would invite me in and then maybe I'd ask her out on a date.*
> Why?
> *Because I really like her, but she obviously doesn't feel the same.*
> Why?
> *Because she didn't invite me inside. Now I feel rejected.*

Give it a go. Keep your character talking and don't let them off the hook until they reveal the truth and you have the information you need to progress your scene effectively.

The Age of Aquarius

'Not from the stars do I my judgement pluck,
and yet methinks I have astronomy.'

Sonnet 14, *William Shakespeare*

In Sonnet 14, the Bard wrote that whilst he thought he had a handle on astronomy, he didn't let it guide him or help him to make predictions. However, if you look at Ancient Greek mythology, the connections to the western Zodiac are clear. The word 'Zodiac' itself derives from Ancient Greek, meaning 'circle of little animals'.

Ares (Aries) was the Greek god of war, son of Zeus and Hera, and brother to Athena. He is believed to be Aphrodite's lover, scorned by her husband. Character traits linked to the star sign today include being untamed and highly passionate. Aphrodite herself (Taurus) is the goddess of love and beauty. The daughter of Jupiter, she had three children by Ares and was believed to be a social butterfly, overindulgent, with a taste for the finer things in life. Today, traits of those born under the Taurus star sign are said to be creative and passionate and often dramatic. Whether you see yourself as a believer or a sceptic, the twelve different star signs represented in the Zodiac provide a simple way to look at a tableau of twelve different archetypes… just like the cast of characters in a script. So, if you want to write the next Oedipus or Medea, give the following astrological writing exercise a try.

Start by writing down two or three brand-new character names and assign each of them a different star sign (see list over the page). Next, look up their daily horoscope, either online or in a newspaper. Using the astrologer's prediction as a jumping-off point for a story, apply the information in each character's horoscope to inspire a single scene.

Tomorrow, return to the same source and read each of the character horoscopes again, using this update to guide the next scene, and so on. Continue this for as long as you wish, allowing the stars to guide the characters' decisions as the story unfolds.

Zodiac achetypes

ᐯ *Aries*: Eager, dynamic, quick and competitive.

♉ *Taurus*: Strong, dependable, sensual and creative.

♊ *Gemini*: Versatile, expressive, curious and kind.

♋ *Cancer*: Intuitive, sentimental, compassionate and protective.

♌ *Leo*: Dramatic, outgoing, fiery and self-assured.

♍ *Virgo*: Practical, loyal, gentle and analytical.

♎ *Libra*: Social, fair-minded, diplomatic and gracious.

♏ *Scorpio*: Passionate, stubborn, resourceful and brave.

♐ *Sagittarius*: Extroverted, optimistic, funny and generous.

♑ *Capricorn*: Serious, independent, disciplined and tenacious.

♒ *Aquarius*: Deep, imaginative, original and uncompromising.

♓ *Pisces*: Affectionate, empathetic, wise and artistic.

The Absent Protagonist

In writing my verbatim dramas, The Countess (*Blue Elephant Theatre, London, 2016*) *and* In the Tall Grass (*Bishop Arts Theatre Center, Dallas, 2017*)*, the characters at the heart of each story were absent from the script. In the curious case of Marianne Johnson, aka Countess Mariaska Romanov, the Brent Council benefit thief declined to be involved in the project. In Texas, however, Shade Schuler, a murdered transgender woman of colour, was no longer alive and able to tell her story.*

Writing verbatim plays in which the central characters were unable to contribute presented a challenge. How could I make their presence felt on stage, and not have the audience feel as though something was missing? Ethically, how could I ensure balanced viewpoints were being presented without their voices? In The Countess, *rich interviews with friends in the community, exclusive information from the fraud investigation team at Brent Council and news sources were presented alongside court transcripts, including testimony from Johnson herself, which was then spoken on stage by a different member of the chorus each time we heard from Johnson – a nod to the numerous aliases assumed by the serial fraudster. With* In the Tall Grass, *a highly emotional interview from Josh Schuler, Shade's brother, at the eleventh hour allowed greater access to Shade herself and added new depth to the material already gathered from close friends within the community.*

I quickly found that establishing how a character is perceived by others can give them an air of mystery, making the character and their story all the more interesting for the audience whilst heightening anticipation and suspense.

Richard II and Richard III aside, William Shakespeare introduced all of his tragic heroes to the audiences prior to their arrival on stage. The title character in The Wizard of Oz *is probably the best-known example of a character whose presence is felt for the majority of the story, whom the central quest will be resolved by, yet whom we don't meet until the very end. Worshipped by his subjects, believing he is the only man capable of solving their problems, the perceptions and expectations set-up by other characters are what drive our thoughts and feelings about the wizard before we even meet him. With an otherworldly reputation successfully established, the only possible feeling for Dorothy and her chums when they finally meet the (not so) great and powerful man behind the curtain is disappointment.*

What is it they say? Never meet your idols?

Write a scene in which your protagonist is only present through the candid descriptions of him/her/them by others. Think about:

- What information you can impart to the audience about your protagonist that they might not otherwise be willing or able to share themselves?

- How can you use other characters to subvert the audience's opinions or feelings about your protagonist?

- How can your protagonist's thoughts, feelings, opinions and 'voice' be heard despite their absence?

- Fundamentally, how do we still feel the character's presence through their absence?

For a moving study of an absent protagonist on screen, see Carol Morley's 2011 documentary/drama *Dreams of a Life*, which tells the story of Joyce Vincent, a young woman whose skeleton was discovered in her London bedsit three years after she had died.

Flaws and All

Just as we are all affected by change and shaped by our life experiences, our characters should be products of their environments too. Our protagonists don't have to be perfectly polished model citizens – in fact, it is their imperfections and flaws that stop them from being boring and predictable. Some of the most notable characters of all time have emerged from the trial and tribulations of life, having survived to live another day... flaws and all.

Looking at the backstory of a character from one of your own projects, can you pinpoint an event, moment or feeling that might have led them to an opinion, fear or sensibility that manifests within the pages of your script and guides their actions or feelings?

- As a child, did they overhear a parent repeatedly complain about being overweight, which has led to body issues in their own life? Or perhaps they are of the belief that heavier people are inferior and this manifests in their disdain or attitude towards another character?

- Has the character been overlooked for promotion or love on several occasions, which has led to feelings of jealousy or resentment?

- If they were raised in a family with very little money, do they now place higher importance on wealth and success over friendship, love and true happiness? Or is the opposite true?

- Or perhaps they are the last single person in a friendship circle which has led to them feeling bitter or belligerent?

If you struggle to define a moment in a character's backstory, then try the exercise in reverse. Decide on a past event with emotional, poignant or dramatic potential and assign this to the character. Knowing this new piece of information about them might affect their story, interactions with other characters, as well as their wants and desires.

Don't be afraid to give a good character a seemingly negative trait. We all bear the scars, memories and notches of life. This makes us resilient, it is how we grow, develop, learn and move forward. This doesn't define us as bad people, less heroic or weaker… it just adds texture and makes us real. Just like an old piece of furniture, sometimes chipping away at the edges or distressing certain features can highlight the detail and add real depth and value to a character.

Daddy or Chips?

If you lived in the UK in the 1990s, you will no doubt remember the TV commercial from McCain Oven Chips, in which little Sophie's older sister poses the question, 'What do you like best, Daddy or chips?' If you didn't, search for it online. The question sparks inner conflict for Sophie, who mulls over the dilemma all the way until tea time when her daddy stops by the dining table to swipe an oven chip from her plate, helping her to make up her mind.

Internal conflict is a great tool for us as writers and can add excitement or intrigue for the audience, presenting a moral, ethical or emotional challenge for our protagonist in place of what might otherwise be a straightforward decision. For example:

> *Matt has been asked to travel to San Diego with a wildlife charity, to campaign for the release of two orcas from an aquarium. However, his wife is on the board of governors at the international pharmaceutical company who sell sedatives to the aquarium to stabilise the mental health of their captive whales.*

> *If this story were to play out, what are Matt's options? Does he go to San Diego at the expense of harming his wife's career and potentially risking his marriage? Or does he turn down the opportunity to take a stand and fight for something he passionately believes in?*

By forcing our protagonists to confront or contradict their own belief system, or to act against their own morality, ethics or better judgement, we can add internal conflict to their character arc. This, in turn, raises the stakes and heightens the drama.

Think about the following moral dilemmas from the perspective of your protagonist (or invent other appropriate ones)... how would they respond?

- The representative from a charity calls to thank you for a very generous donation that you didn't make. They want to ask if you will take part in a promotional campaign as one of their most valued donors. Do you accept the invitation, or tell the truth?

- You see an estranged acquaintance from the past arrive at your office for an interview in your department. You would rather not have to catch up, let alone work alongside them. Do you rubbish their name to ruin their chances, or suck it up?

- You are a passenger in your father's car. At a junction, he fails to see a cyclist, knocking them to the ground. Would you be willing to commit perjury and testify that your father was driving carefully, blaming the cyclist instead?

- Money talks. How much would be enough to convince you to take a loyal, healthy pet to the vet to be put to sleep? They say everyone has a price!

- You bump into an old flame with whom you have no interest in reconnecting. They invite you to an expensive restaurant that you have been dying to visit. Do you go?

In which direction does your protagonist's moral compass point? Could internal conflict for your characters be strengthened by presenting them with an ethical or moral question?

See *Exercise 2.6: One Step Forward*, another exercise to explore conflict.

In Loving Memory

'On Tuesday, June 19, Valerie Macintosh, tea lady, dog groomer and Avon delivery lady, passed away at the age of 65. Valerie is survived by her whippet, Sophie, a Kenwood sandwich toaster, and a pile of ironing.'

One way to see your characters more clearly, whether you are in the process of creating a new character or trying to clarify aspects of an established one, is to view their life retrospectively by writing their obituary. In doing so, you will be able to review their impact, relationships, highs, lows – and consider if they had their time again, what might they change? What might they do differently?

Use the pointers below to pen an obituary for one of your characters. You can either do this from your own perspective, as the creator of the character and their world, or from the perspective of an associated character who may or may not appear in your script – e.g. a close friend or relative of the character. Keep in mind that a good obituary will usually acknowledge loss and express pain whilst remembering a life and the unique qualities of the deceased. It needn't be depressing and gloomy – you can reflect the character of the person and look back on their life with wit and affection.

Begin by announcing their death, including their name, age and the date of their passing, followed by a brief mention of loved ones left behind. The example of the top of the page is how I might start to remember Valerie, a beloved Lancashire tea lady who featured in my sketch comedies *Tickled Pink!* and *MCN TV!*

Go on to share more biographical information relating to their childhood, early life, education, achievements and career.

Defining these kinds of details will help, particularly when creating new characters and working out their backstories. You might also mention any marriages or enduring relationships here.

In the next paragraph, try to capture the spirit of your character, thinking about what motivated them, their interests, hobbies, passions, contributions to society, as well as any character traits that were unique to them. Think about the character traits that the people around them are likely to remember fondly (or otherwise) and try to make it personal – will they be remembered for their quick wit, infectious laugh or their sarcasm? It's not a biography, so the trick is to find a balance between writing a meaningful tribute whilst conveying the character's personality.

Digging a little deeper, perhaps there is information about their character that has only come to light following their death, which might be helpful for you to know whilst writing your script. Were they a secret philanthropist? Do they have illegitimate children who might have come forward now in order to pay their respects? Again, they might not feature in the script you are writing, but knowing this information about your character will inform their backstory and may affect the decisions or choices they make, or the way they avoid or respond to specific events or topics of conversation.

In closing, include funeral details, as well as information regarding donations, flowers or condolences. Perhaps your character had a favourite flower, a dress code they have instructed for their 'celebration of life', or maybe donations to the local cat sanctuary have been requested.

Additionally, or alternatively, consider a self-written obituary. Imagining your character was aware of their impending death and wanted to control the narrative of their life, what would they write, and how might it differ from how others would remember them?

Speed-Dating

First impressions count, and you learn a lot about a person in the first two minutes of meeting them. Harvard Business School professor Amy Cuddy has been studying first impressions for more than fifteen years and in her study of communication, found that we make instant decisions about people based on their eye contact, appearance and their handshake, as well as the verbal and non-verbal cues they give. Cuddy says people quickly answer two questions when they first meet you: 'Can I trust this person?' and 'Can I respect this person?'

Whilst we can't always meet our characters in real life, by 'hot-seating' the characters in your script, you can cut out the small-talk and really get to know who they are, and what makes them tick in a short space of time. Speed-dating is an ideal way to get up close and personal with your characters! You may learn new information that will strengthen your knowledge and understanding of them, as you build their story on the page.

For this practical exercise, start by placing two chairs opposite one another. Next, set a series of back-to-back, five-minute timers on your phone, enough for each of the characters in your script and prop the next page open on one of the chairs.

Assuming the role of your first character, sit in the empty chair and start the timer. From the perspective of your character, try to answer as many of the following 'getting to know you' questions as you can in five minutes. When the time runs out, switch to a new character and rerun the questions.

I find it useful to stand when the timer chimes and walk around the chairs before sitting back down in the other seat. Switching from one chair to the other aids switching between 'dates', both physically and mentally. You may also want to make a quick audio or video recording of each 'date', allowing you to embody each of your characters fully without having to write things down.

1. What book are you reading at the moment?
2. If you won the lottery, how would you spend it?
3. What makes you laugh?
4. Is religion important to you?
5. What are your political beliefs?
6. Where do you see yourself in five years?
7. What are you most passionate about?
8. What do you consider to be your best attributes?
9. If you could have three wishes, what would they be?
10. What has been your proudest moment?
11. Do you see the glass as half-full or half-empty?
12. If you could change one thing about yourself, what would it be?
13. What are the most important things you look for in a person?
14. What song best sums you up?
15. What's the most reckless thing you've ever done?
16. What is the most adventurous thing you've ever done?
17. If you could have dinner with three people living or dead, who would they be?
18. What is your idea of a perfect vacation?
19. What is the craziest thing you would do for love?
20. What would be the title of your biography?

You probably won't have time to ask more than ten questions in five minutes, assuming thirty-second answers, so pick the issues that seem most relevant when meeting each character. Keep it frenetic and don't overthink it.

Revisit this exercise during your writing process if you have questions for your characters, or want to drill down or grill them about any backstory details or areas you need clarity on. You might even want to write specific questions, asking them in the role of another character in your script, to gain a better understanding of their motivation in a particular scene, e.g.:

- Why can't you tell Emma you loved her? What are you afraid of?

- What Melissa just said to you wasn't kind. Why do you let her talk to you like that?

- Your actions at the dinner table left your sister heartbroken. Why do you find if so difficult to admit when you've made a mistake?

The Day the Characters Quit

One of the great joys of being a parent has got to be bedtime. But before we kick back and fall asleep in front of Netflix… there is the pleasure of reading to a little person. If so, you may have come across a delightful picturebook by American author and filmmaker Drew Daywalt called The Day the Crayons Quit. *If not, I highly suggest you read it, as well as the sequel,* The Day the Crayons Came Home; *even for adults these stories are really imaginative and fun, filled with good humor and positive messages.*

In his books, Daywalt gives each colour in the crayon box a distinct voice as they pen resignation letters to their poor owner, Duncan, who just wants to do his colouring. In turn, Duncan's crayons address their concerns: blue crayon is overworked and short and stubby as a result, green crayon is tired of being used to colour trees and dinosaurs, and the orange and yellow crayons are no longer speaking to each other as they disagree on which is the actual colour of the sun.

My sons love these books and we read them again and again, which gave me an idea for a writing exercise. What if the characters in one of my scripts quit in a similar fashion? What would their grievances be with me as their creator? Would they object to the manner in which I divulge their backstories? The romantic relations in which I embroil them? Or what about the times I have allowed another character to speak to them without providing an appropriate opportunity for them to respond? Perhaps they would like more lines in one scene… or to be left out of certain scenes altogether?

Take one of your own scripts and have your characters write resignation monologues. Index cards are great for this, allowing you just a few minutes writing for each character and making it an ideal warm-up exercise. However, if you are feeling inspired or your character's concerns or demands start you on a roll, then go for it… why stop at a postcard?

Finally… be open to the possibility that your characters might just raise some valid points which you have not previously considered? Is there merit in their madness? If you choose a character from a work in progress, then hold on to these postcards and reflect on their arguments when you approach your next draft.

DIALOGUE

'Don't tell me the Moon is shining;
show me the glint of light on broken glass.'

Anton Chekhov

The best way to write real dialogue is to make it engaging, authentic and believable for real people to listen to, and to have it sound like real people are talking. How do we do that? Easy! We listen to how real people talk. Conversations are going on all around us. In terms of believability, often the way in which people speak is more important than what they are actually saying. You will find exercises in this part which look at how to tune in to real conversations and capture the essence of a voice on the page, focusing on the unique and distinctive styles which characterise dialogue.

It is often said that less is more when it comes to dialogue, so I have also included a couple of exercises that look at boiling scenes down to their hot topics, identifying the primary purpose or function of each scene. Often this can be achieved through visual storytelling too. Remember, you are writing for a visual medium, so why have a character unnecessarily say or explain something that can be seen or shown, either physically or through actions or emotions?

THE ELEMENTS

Unique Voice

Part of writing great dialogue is ensuring each character has a unique voice, with character-specific dialogue. A quick way to determine if you have achieved this with any script is to delete the character names and read the dialogue aloud. Can you still tell who is saying what? Or could any of your characters have that conversation with the same outcome? If your dialogue is generic enough that almost any of your characters could speak the lines, then spend some time getting to know your characters and connecting with them on a deeper level.

Pick one scenario and three of the characters from the lists opposite. Write a short, one- or two-page scene, paying attention to each character's unique word choices, their rhythm of speech, the tone of their voice, and if appropriate, any accent, dialect or speech pattern you feel they might have. Consider if their speech might be fast and exhausting, or slow and deliberate. Do they add words like 'like' or 'right' in the middle of their speech? Do they throw in exclamations at the end of their sentences, such as 'know what I mean?' Or 'Amen!', which characterise their speech in a way that is unique to them.

Sometimes what a character doesn't say can reveal more about how they feel than what they do say, so also think about anything that might be best left unsaid!

By limiting the scene to a single, enclosed location, with little action, this exercise allows you to focus on the dialogue and ensure it is specific and personal to each character. I have left the character descriptions brief so that there is room for creativity here.

Scenarios

- In a small motel bar, three travellers watch the lottery draw live on television. In unison, they check their tickets. They have each won large amounts. How does, or doesn't, each character reveal the big news?

- At an airport, three passengers with luggage take the lift from the car park to the departures terminal. The lift lights go out, and it stops moving. One of them calls for help, but it's several hours before they are freed.

- Three strangers attending an assertiveness workshop are left waiting in a small classroom when their instructor's car breaks down, and she is delayed by a couple of hours.

- Arriving early for their driving tests, three learner drivers sit in a holding room awaiting their instructors when they are informed that two of the centre's instructors have called in sick. It will be at least ninety minutes before the one remaining instructor returns.

- Three attendees at an anger-management retreat are left stranded at a campsite on the top of a mountain when heavy snowfall cuts off the only road in or out. Staff at the cabin below advise they must camp out for another night until a snowplough arrives.

Characters

- Luke, an aspirational young air steward from a poor family.

- Denise, a wealthy venture capitalist with homes in various countries.

- Sian, a veteran writer, currently penning a trilogy of vampire novels.

- Karen, an ex-con turned good who runs a vegan bakery.

THE ELEMENTS

- Mikey, a pro-motocross rider who has recently lost both of his legs in an accident.

As an extension of this exercise, why not write a short diary entry from each of the three characters' point of view, about the events of the scene. Writing a diary is a great way to hear a character's unique voice by way of internal monologue.

Lady of the House Speaking

'If there's one thing I can't stand, it's snobbery and
one-upmanship. People trying to pretend they're superior.
Makes it so much harder for those of us who really are.'

Hyacinth Bucket in Keeping Up Appearances *by Roy Clarke*

*From time to time, most of us would admit that we are guilty of
changing what we say, or the way in which we speak, depending
on to whom we are talking. For instance, at a job interview, we
are likely to be conscious of presenting the best possible image of
ourselves to make a good impression and land the role. Likewise,
when speaking to a lawyer, doctor, university professor or similar
professional person. Since most of us adjust our speech to suit
our audience, we are likely to relax our speech and give a more
honest representation of our true selves when ordering coffee, or
speaking to a blue-collar service professional. A lasting memory of
my lovely nana, Dot, is her 'la-di-da' Hyacinth Bucket (which the
character always pronounces 'Bouquet') telephone voice – a
pretence she would quickly drop once she realised it was a family
member on the other end of the line.*

Write both sides of two short telephone conversations, one
where your protagonist is speaking to a stranger in a
professional or formal situation; and another in which they are
talking to a loved one or close friend. Have them covey the
same information and notice how their speech changes. The
former will likely be a filtered version of themselves and the
latter, more relaxed and natural.

Here are some example scenarios:

* Following a job interview your character wants to
  celebrate. First, they call their recruitment agent with the
  news. Next, they call their partner or a parent.

- The council have given your character the keys to a vacant shop to run a pop-up café during a literary festival. First, they call their business partner. Next, they speak to a local news reporter.

- Your character has decided to leave their home in Yorkshire and move with their small children to Miami. First, they call their employer, then they must call their parents.

I'm Not Being Funny, *But…*

George Bernard Shaw said, 'Silence is the most perfect expression of scorn.' *He also said,* 'Every line has a bullet in it and comes with an explosion.'

Have you ever been in a situation where someone is desperate to have an argument with you? No matter how you try to defuse the situation, they want to pick a fight? Sometimes, people are just plain aggressive, but for others, passive aggression might be their weapon of choice. Finding it hard for whatever reason to just come out and say whatever it is that they want/need, they beat around the bush, or even cause an argument, the crux of which is engineered to reveal their real agenda.

This usually manifests in one of two ways: overtly or covertly. Overt passive aggression may be one person giving the other the silent treatment – refusing to respond to civil questions or to engage in discussion. This makes it evident that they are upset about something, with the desire being for the other person to react. Whereas covert passive aggression might look like a phone call not returned, lame excuses, or just being purposefully unhelpful or counterproductive.

With Shaw's words of wisdom in mind, write a scene between two people, one hurting or angry, the other refusing to be drawn into an argument. The only rule is that they are not allowed to speak frankly. Instead, think about how they use veiled threats and passive aggression to convey their thoughts and feelings.

Here are a few suggestions for your scene:

A character might say one thing but clearly mean another. You know, those clichéd lines that people tend to use in place of what they really mean, or to hide what they really mean…

- To be honest… (I am either not being honest, or trying to add weight to my opinion.)

- I'm not being rude/funny but… (I am totally being rude and/or funny.)

- I'm just saying… *or* No offence, but… (I'm trying to make my insult seem socially acceptable.)

- I hope you don't mind, but… (I'm going to say or do it anyway.)

- …only joking! (I am not joking, in any way, shape or form.)

- Don't worry, I'll do it. (I am annoyed because you are not doing it to my liking.)

- Yeah, I'm fine. (I'm not fine, and my face and body language say it all.)

Generalising is another way. Often people will make broad statements that attempt to claim that their thoughts or feelings are shared by others, with lines like:

- I've heard some people are saying…

- I'm not the only one who thinks this.

- People might not like it if you…

- I'm just trying to protect you from…

For a masterclass in writing this type of dialogue, watch the films in Helen Fielding's *Bridget Jones* trilogy! Emotionally charged, yet subtle. Also, read *The Birthday Party*, to see how Harold Pinter slowly builds the torment of Stanley by McCann and Goldberg.

I'll Join You for Dessert

'Enter a conversation as late as you can.'

Aaron Sorkin

Wordy dialogue and too much exposition can be the death of a scene. I had a crash-course in getting into a scene as quickly as possible when writing for the American docudrama series, The Price of Fame. *The very nature of the docudrama genre dictates that whatever you write in terms of scripted drama will be fighting for screen time with talking-head interviews. With a brief to include around thirty dramatic scenes in each episode of the show, I soon learnt that every word counts and there is no room for superfluous set-up.*

I call this exercise I'll Join You for Dessert – *the school of thought being that appetisers and entrées only serve to present unnecessary fluff and fail to move a scene forward. When you are writing on commission and need to deliver a script of precise length, you need to cut to the chase… or to dessert in this case. It's the sweetest bit and is probably where the crux of the scene lies.*

First, print out a copy of one scene from your script. Next, write down a single word at the top of the page in capital letters, defining the purpose of the scene in your play or screenplay. Is it to SET-UP? To REVEAL? To CHALLENGE? To ENTRAP? To RESOLVE? Whatever the purpose, a good scene must advance the story in some way. Now read your scene and identify one single line of dialogue in the scene where the keyword which you have identified at the top of the page occurs. Having done so, question if any of the dialogue that is written before this line helps to advance your story in any way? Or does it instead stop you from 'getting into the scene' quicker? Perhaps cutting *every* line before the key line might be a step too far… but think hard, and question the purpose of unnecessary dialogue.

Talk is cheap, but rambling might cost you. It is said that writing is rewriting, which may well be true. Rewriting, or specifically, editing for me, is one of the hardest parts of the job. It is much harder to be objective and dogmatic when trying to trim, tighten and make our scripts as lean as they can be. Whilst an exercise like this may seem brutal, its simple focus will help you to define and remember the purpose of each scene, in turn helping you to see the wood for the trees. You will be better positioned to make the tough decisions that will ultimately make your writing the best that it can be.

Sell It, Don't Tell It

3.2.
5

Unless we are writing a period piece, talking in tongues or writing in verse, for the most part we want our dialogue to sound natural. That's the aim. But dialogue has a job to do; it is not just idle chit-chat, it must convey important information about character and story to the audience. So, how do we make our dialogue play out organically, in such a way that it feels personal to the character, instead of imparting information like an infomercial?

One way to make dialogue serve its purpose whilst sounding natural is to show, *not* tell *the action. I know… 'show, don't tell', it's the first rule of writing, but all too often it is also the first rule to be broken. Put simply, you never want to have a character say they are angry, sad, excited or nervous. You need to show the emotion through the character's action. Likewise, in revealing a critical piece of information about a character, never have one character say to another, 'So, Mike… Shirley tells me you're a mechanic?' Having Mike enter in dirty overalls and go straight to the kitchen sink to wash his hands is one way to avoid this. Remember that stage and screen are visual mediums, so use this exercise to look closely at dialogue which really should be written as a stage direction or screenplay action instead.*

Here are three exercises to practise the principle of showing, not telling:

- Write a short scene between two friends. Assign each of them a specific occupation and find a way to reveal what these are to the audience without either of them saying what their job is. Sure, they can talk about their day at work or aspects of their career, but the action and the interaction between the characters should let us connect the dots and figure out what their jobs are.

- Write a short scene between an ex-boss and employee which conveys their connection, without them saying that they used to work together.

- Write a short scene between a former couple. How can you show the audience that they have a history and were previously involved without stating the fact?

We Are What We Speak

Nothing is more jarring to watch as an audience member than an actor speaking dialogue which doesn't sound natural to their character. It is the job of the writer to craft character-specific dialogue within the element of the character – not to be confused with writing stereotypes. Every character needs dialogue appropriate to their age, education, life experience, social class and so forth.

Pick a character from your work and have a go at rewriting the lines of dialogue below so that they suit your character. Think about the words that your character would use, the rhythm of their speech, any slang words or dialect that might be specific to them. Would they speak in full and complete sentences, or would their dialogue be broken or trail off? Would they use metaphors, flowery language or be short, sharp and direct? Try to capture a snapshot of your character through the way in which they convey the meaning behind each line.

Dialogue

- I had coffee with him yesterday. He was… I don't know. Different.

- Wait. Just sit down for a minute, there's something I need to tell you.

- I'm so over this, I just need a break. I'm thinking of taking a year out to travel.

Listening In

The best way to write real dialogue is to listen to real conversations. I mean really listen. The way people speak can reveal so much about them. Our voice (incorporating vocabulary, accent, dialect, rhythm of speech and delivery) is just as distinct to each of us as our fingerprint or face.

When I am writing verbatim dramas, I spend extended periods conducting interviews and doing immersive research (more on this in Part 4). During the interview stage of the process, I become a sponge, literally soaking up every word and nuance of each of my subjects' stories as I record hours and hours of interviews.

The next stage of the process is transcribing – the process of manually 'downloading' the recorded interviews from a digital file on my Dictaphone into a text document. I am always keen to include every false start, stutter, repeated word and the uniqueness of my subjects' speech, in order to capture the minute details of their voice and present a work on stage whereby the audience hear the words as though first-hand. As such, transcribing interviews usually takes between ten to fifteen minutes for every minute of recorded time as I rewind tiny sections of audio, again and again, to check I have accurately captured every single breath, 'umm', 'like', 'err' and 'so'.

Whilst most naturalistic scripts won't call for this level of irregularity in their dialogue, listening to real speech and dissecting it in this manner helps to strengthen the connection between the way words sound when being spoken, and the way they are written and read; thus improving your dialogue-to-speech dexterity. It's a bit like taking a working clock, opening it up to see how the insides work and then putting it back together again. Of course, this technique is not just useful when writing a verbatim drama; time spent listening acutely to how people talk to each other is a great way to improve your general dialogue writing.

THE ELEMENTS

Take yourself off to a place where you might naturally overhear a conversation between two people. This doesn't need to be anything terribly exciting – sometimes the most dreary or mundane exchanges are the best in terms of capturing real-world conversational dialogue. Suggested locations might include:

DIALOGUE

- A launderette, since you can easily sit and scribble whilst waiting for your laundry.

- A café where you can nurse a coffee for an extended period whilst eavesdropping.

- A bus or train. Listening to other passengers chatting openly is easy to do.

Laws differ in different parts of the world, but it is safe to assume that it is almost always illegal to record a private conversation that you are not party to. So, for the purpose of this exercise, take along a notebook and pen.

Listen to a conversation for ten or fifteen minutes and just scribble away, capturing as much of the conversation as you can without stopping. Don't worry about writing character names each time a different person speaks, simply start a new line and keep writing. The idea here is to tune in to the way in which each of the people speak, their phrasing and rhythm. Likewise, don't worry about capturing the whole conversation if you can't write fast enough, just look at this as a freewriting exercise (see *Exercise 2.1: Freewriting/Freetalking* on page 14) in which you will simply fill a few pages with a stream of raw dialogue as you hear it.

Here are a few things to listen out for:

- Each person's individual manner and speech style (e.g. dry, technical, long-winded).

- Their pitch, tone and the rhythm of their delivery (e.g. monotonous, excitable).

- Their word choices and vocabulary (e.g. long words, slang, old-fashioned).

- How they start and finish a sentence (e.g. do they complete or trail off?).

- The use of any idiosyncrasies that are specific and unique to them.

- If their voices overlap and talk over each other.

When your time is up, leave the location and take a walk for fifteen minutes. Find a quiet place to sit and go back to your notebook.

Now, with the voices of the two people in your head, read your writing aloud to yourself, replaying the scene you just captured. You should now be attuned to the way each of the two voices speak and interact with one another. Next, turn to a blank page and write for ten minutes. Imagining if you had not got off the bus, left the launderette or café, how would the next ten minutes of the conversation play out? Don't worry too much about the content of the conversation or the characters involved; instead remember the nature and style of the dialogue and just try to keep writing in the voices of the real people.

Talking in Incomplete...

Word-processing software can be annoying for a scriptwriter. How many times have you written a line of wonderfully snappy dialogue only to have that annoying line appear underneath your words, labelling your writing 'fragmented' or 'grammatically incorrect'? Software likes us to conform to proper sentence structure, and write in complete sentences. However, in real life, people don't always... Right? So why should dialogue in a script be any...

Don't be afraid to use sentence fragments. Truly naturalistic dialogue is filled with incomplete sentences and meandering thoughts, especially in a situation where characters interact informally. In fact, in a relaxed, familiar or casual setting, characters will usually interrupt and talk past one another.

Here are three writing exercises, each designed to inspire a quick dialogue exchange. Have a go at writing casual, fragmented dialogue that would be considered incomplete by the recognised laws of language.

- *Different goals*: Write a scene in which a couple both want different things. e.g. One person wants to meet up with another couple and go to the movies, whilst the other wants just the two of them to go out for a quiet dinner.

  - *Think about how strongly each character is prepared to state their case and how a heated exchange might alter the way they speak to each other.*

- *Different knowledge*: Write a scene in which one character knows more about something than the other. e.g. A young driver takes their car to the garage to figure out why a warning light has started blinking. The mechanic knows why and begins to talk in detail about the car's on-board computer system and the reasons behind the warning light, whilst the driver just wants to know how much it will cost to fix and how long it will take.

○ *If the driver is disinterested and/or in a hurry to leave, their dialogue should reflect this. Perhaps it will be a little curt and hurried.*

• **Different secrets**: Write a scene in which two characters each have a secret which they want to keep from each other at all costs. e.g. A son comes home and wants to go to the shed to smoke pot; however, his father is hiding his mistress in the shed.

○ *The son can't reveal why he wants to go to the shed, and must stop his father from finding his secret stash. Likewise, the father can't explain why he doesn't want his son to go to the shed. This scenario has the potential for very awkward dialogue, with comic and/or tragic potential. Are the characters open, warm and friendly whilst covering up their lies, or aloof and abrupt with one another?*

Sometimes in playwriting, but more so in screenwriting – particularly when writing for soap or serial drama where there is little or no time for the actors to rehearse before shooting a scene – we write a thought or unspoken word in parentheses for clarity and speed. *For example...*

                    TRACEY
    Hey, I thought we were... (having
    lunch together)

                    SONIA
    We are.

                    TRACEY
    Then why... (is he here?)

                    SONIA
    Sit down. His treat!

Try this approach when writing your scene. The parentheses can always be deleted later, but may help you to clarify your intentions.

You Sound Familiar?!

What if you find yourself in a position where you are writing for a soap opera or serial drama, where the well-established characters are not your own creation but are just as familiar and well known as a close family member? Soap-opera viewers invite the residents of fictional streets, neighbourhoods or hospitals into their lives nightly and become quickly invested in the highs and lows of their dramatic lives. I watched a whole year of the New Zealand soap Shortland Street *before starting to write for the show, listening hard to become familiar with each of the core cast and their individual dialogue profiles.*

Writing for existing characters is a useful skill for all writers to add to their toolbox, not least those who aspire to write continuing drama. A common misconception is that writers on a soap or serial drama only write for one or two characters, getting to know their voice and in turn how to write their character-specific dialogue. In fact, dialogue writers are commissioned on a per-episode basis and write complete episodes. The story arc of those episodes is prescribed by the 'storyline document', a fifteen- to seventeen-page prose document which is created by the storyline writers following the weekly story conference.

*Thinking about UK soap operas, as that was my primary exposure during my formative years, each of the big three (*EastEnders, Coronation Street *and* Emmerdale) *have their own distinct regional 'voices'. By this, I mean not only the regional dialects and accents that separate the East End of London from Manchester and the Yorkshire Dales, but the culture, style, tone and any socio-economic factors which are unique to these places and which are therefore ingrained in the storytelling.*

The following scenario is an example scene that might be provided to you in a storyline document:

Jason visits Meaghan to discuss the divorce papers. Meaghan's still feeling conflicted and admits it's all happening very fast. Jason points out she was the one who initiated proceedings. He's happy to keep things the way they are – he doesn't want to end their marriage, and he knows their son Deon feels the same. However, he is resigned in that he wants Meaghan to be happy and if this is what she wants, he'll sign. His understanding only makes Meaghan feel more confused, and she admits she's unsure.

Your challenge is to apply this given scene to two different on-screen couples, writing the scene in their voices. First, pick two fictional couples with whom you are familiar, past or present – this might be, for example, Jimmy and Jackie Corkhill from *Brookside*, Susan and Karl Kennedy from *Neighbours*, or Ross and Rachel from *Friends*. Watch back some of their classic scenes on YouTube and really try to get inside the heads and tune in to their distinct voices, as well as the overall 'voice' and style of their programmes. As you watch, jot down any notes relating to the rhythm of their speech and any verbal characteristics. Study one couple at a time, making your notes and then writing the scene.

If writing for soap is something that interests you, then why not write a spec script based on your favourite show and send it to the Script Producer, expressing your interest and demonstrating your talents?

For further reading on this specific genre, I wholly recommend Chris Thompson's book *Writing Soap* (Aber Publishing, 2011) and Yvonne Grace's *Writing for Television: Series, Serials and Soaps* (Creative Essentials, 2014).

Emoji Talk

If a picture is worth a thousand words, the final exercise in this part of the book will have you hitting the ten-thousand-word count in no time. It is quick and addictive!

Translate the following five emoji stories to create quick duologues…

1.

2.

3.

4.

5.

Here is an example:

SCOTT. Ah. (*Checks his pockets.*) Damn. I can't believe it.

RYAN. Forgot your wallet again?

SCOTT. Yeah. Sorry.

RYAN. No worries. You can get the drinks tomorrow night.

SCOTT. Yeah, about that. I don't think I can make it tomorrow.

RYAN. Let me guess… unicorn racing again?!

SCOTT. How about I give you a ride home, and we do something at the weekend?

RYAN. Sure. Whatever.

SCOTT. I'll give you a ring on Friday, yeah?

RYAN. Don't bother. I'll be washing my hair.

Why not try writing an emoji chain story over your favourite messaging app with a fellow writer friend? Start by sending your friend a random emoji, to which they should send back an inspired line of dialogue, along with an emoji of their choice, you reply by turning their emoji into a line of dialogue, and so on.

All emojis designed by OpenMoji (openmoji.org).

SUBTEXT

'Spectators come to the theatre to hear the subtext.
They can read the text at home.'

Konstantin Stanislavsky

If the idea of writing subtext seems a little daunting, then let's break things down and first understand what subtext actually is:

Text = What a character says

Subtext = What a character means

In a nutshell, subtext is the implicit meaning, message or theme in a line of dialogue, scene, or entire play or screenplay. It's how our characters express their feelings in a way that makes our dialogue more dynamic, entertaining and intriguing. You will find a selection of exercises in this part to help add or strengthen the subtext/s within your scripts.

Writing Between the Lines

Take a look at this short piece of dialogue between a mother and her son:

> DENISE
> Why aren't you coming over with
> the kids for lunch on Sunday?
>
> GAV
> Karen's got some work to finish.
>
> DENISE
> Can't you just bring the kids?
> We're not really fussed about
> seeing Karen anyway.
>
> GAV
> Well, to be honest, neither of us
> actually want to come.
>
> DENISE
> I'm disappointed, Gavin. I went
> out of my way to buy extra food
> for you all.
>
> GAV
> I didn't ask you to.

As it stands, the dialogue is very much 'on the nose' – it states exactly what it's about. The conversation is flat and unengaging because there is no mystery and nothing for the reader or the audience to decode. Here is the same conversation, with subtext:

> DENISE
> Your dad and I will miss you and
> the kids on Sunday.
>
> GAV
> Yeah… sorry, Mum. Karen's on a
> deadline at the moment, so…

                    DENISE
Well, that's what we thought. She
might appreciate the peace and
quiet?

                    GAV
Yeah, but I've got a few odd jobs
to get done in the garden too,
while the weather's nice.

                    DENISE
Oh, that's a shame. I bought an
extra leg of lamb.

                    GAV
Will it freeze?

To add subtext to a scene, read your dialogue aloud, and mark-up any lines which:

• Give too much information away.

• Are unsubtle or are too 'on the nose'.

• Make you cringe.

Now start to think about how you might rewrite these lines to:

• Conceal a thought or feeling.

• Subvert the implied meaning.

• Add nuance to the message beneath the line.

Sometimes it helps to take something to pieces and put it back together in order to understand fully how it works.

As an additional exercise, look at a single page of a screenplay or playscript by a writer you admire, and decode the text. Make notes in the margin with a pencil as you identify the subtext, or truth, beneath each line of dialogue.

Elephant in the Room

> '...it will be nice again if I say things are like white elephants,
> and you'll like it?'
>
> *Ernest Hemingway*

Hemingway's Hills Like White Elephants *is a masterclass in implied meaning. The short story (freely available online, published in August 1927) is about an older American man and a young woman having an argument on a Spanish train station platform. As they debate the 'operation' he wants her to have, the word 'abortion' is never directly used.*

Write a short scene in which two characters are prohibited from directly mentioning something. They can talk about anything else at all, but they mustn't mention this one thing. Make every word count and see how nuanced feelings can add both subtext and tension. Here are some ideas to get you started:

- A father and son are on a train from France to Switzerland for a legal assisted suicide. They can talk about the past, the future, the trees, and mountains outside of the carriage window... but they must not directly discuss the reason for the trip.

- A pair of newlywed virgins sip Champagne on the balcony of their honeymoon suite. Both of them feel nervous at the expectations of their first night as a married couple. They can talk about the wedding ceremony, the fabulous reception, and the embarrassing speeches... but not directly about the impending deed.

- Two student backpackers scale the dizzy heights of Kawarau Bridge in Queenstown, New Zealand, ahead of a planned bungee jump. Both are feeling the fear, but they mustn't express this to each other directly.

By going off-point, having your characters talk about anything but the issue at the heart of the scene, you can actually make the point very clear.

Check out the movie *Carol* (2015) by screenwriter Phyllis Nagy, directed by Todd Haynes. In addition to subversive dialogue, Nagy makes use of secret glances, code, and subtle signals to deliver what is a beautifully textured drama about a forbidden love affair between Carol (played by Cate Blanchett) and Therese (Rooney Mara).

Walls Have Ears

The cautionary proverb 'walls have ears' is a warning about potential eavesdroppers and often prompts those involved in a conversation to talk in riddles. My mother used to say this a lot when I was younger, mouthing surreptitious words to her friends and talking in code whenever children were present during a conversation that we were not supposed to hear.

How would the dialogue in a scene differ if you switched the location from a private chat on the sofa between two friends to a café, bar or public space where they might be overheard? Would they still be able to talk freely, or would they filter their words and conceal more information that isn't suitable to be discussed in public? Why not try it and find out?

Take a scene from your project that occurs in a private setting and relocate it, making the dialogue appropriate for the new location. Think about:

- Words, personal names and details that might be avoided for privacy.

- Thoughts and feelings that might be implied rather than stated.

Once you have done this, lift the new dialogue and drop it back into your previous setting. Note the extra layer of complexity you have added to the scene.

I'm Fine. Really

Ah, the old smiling assassin! A passive-aggressive character can be really enjoyable to write. Some of my favourite characters from stage and screen are the sharp-tongued slayers – I'm thinking of Vera in Richard Harris's Stepping Out, *mother and daughter Caroline and Celia in Sally Wainwright's* Last Tango in Halifax; *and both Dolly and Jean in Victoria Wood's* Dinnerladies. *The way all these characters phrase their put-downs and attacks gives them the ability to say hurtful things (their subtext) whilst retaining plausible deniability (in their text).*

Write a scene in which two characters almost have an argument, but the need or desire to retain their relationship prevents them from having an all-out fight. Both are itching for a fight, either through frustration, annoyance or anger at the other, but they keep their aggression passive. The subtext of their dialogue should speak the truth, whilst the text (what they actually say) provides a veil for their venom.

The superficial argument should be about something totally mundane or unimportant (cooking dinner, ironing, cleaning the oven or what to watch on TV), whilst the real target for their acrimony, thus the tension in the scene, should stem from something more weighty.

Here are some ideas for a starting line of dialogue, and the subtext to each. Pick one, or make up your own.

Then decide on the real source of the angst. Sharpen your pencil (and your tongue) and write the scene…

- Gosh. Pink.

  - *Why are you painting his bedroom pink? Is my grandson gay?*

THE ELEMENTS

- I'll just pop these dishes back in the dishwasher.
  - *You haven't washed them properly!*
- Were you going for a rustic look?
  - *Your handywork is shabby, and not to my standards.*

And the Winner is…

From time to time we must all work alongside people we might not choose to be friends with outside of work. However, for the sake of a stress-free workday, an easy life, or simply to remain professional, we keep our feelings to ourselves and just get on with things. Right?

Well, imagine your boss asks you to present a workplace award. Now imagine your least favourite co-worker is to be the recipient of the award. Can you really hide your true feelings about their undeserving win and say nice things when you are asked to present them with the award at the monthly company meeting?

Start by writing down a name for your workplace 'frenemy', and the nature of the award. Next, make a few bullet points detailing your feelings towards them. Perhaps you find them smarmy, self-righteous, egotistical or arrogant? If so, why? Write down the underlying reasons for your feelings. Did they swoop in and take a promotion that you thought you were in line for? Did they outperform you? Does your boss view them through rose-tinted glasses? Are they just lazy or bad at their job? Finally, write your award presentation speech. How can you congratulate your colleague with all the sincerity of a congratulating co-worker, whilst the subtext of your address says otherwise?

As an additional exercise, try applying the same technique to a wedding speech. Imagine you are the brother or sister of the bride or groom. How can you pen the perfect toast which demonstrates your dislike and disdain for your new in-law through the gritted teeth of a seething sibling?

THE ELEMENTS

Silence Speaks Volumes

'Drama is life with all the boring bits cut out.'

Alfred Hitchcock

Arrive late, leave early! Just as we talked about getting into a scene as soon as possible (see Exercise 3.2.4: I'll Join You for Dessert on page 79), it is equally important to get out of a scene before it comes to a slow… slow… (s-l-o-w-!!) natural… stop. One way to do this, whilst adding suspense and heightening the subtext, is to leave a fundamental question unanswered. This allows your audience to read between the lines and it keeps things interesting. Remember… silence speaks volumes, so why have your characters provide neat and conclusive answers to every question. Sometimes you can reveal more about their true thoughts by what they don't say.

Look at this example scene:

> NIKHIL WATCHES SPORT ON TV WHILST LACEY FOLDS LAUNDRY. SHE PICKS UP A BABYGROW AND SMELLS IT, HOLDING IT CLOSE.
>
> LACEY
> So, what do you think?
>
> NIKHIL
> Hey?
>
> LACEY
> Another baby, Nik. What do you think?
>
> NIKHIL
> I'm just watching the game, alright?
>
> LACEY
> We talked about having a big family. We've both got siblings.

```
        I thought we wanted the same
        for Ash?
```

Now look at the following edit:

```
                    LACEY
        So, what do you think?

                    NIKHIL
        Hey?

                    LACEY
        Another baby, Nik. What do you
        think?

    ENGROSSED, HE IGNORES HER.

    PAUSE.

                    LACEY
        This laundry won't iron itself.
```

Lacey's devastation is still apparent, without Nikhil having even answered her question. His silence is probably more potent than his answer would have been.

Create a scenario like the one above, with one character asking a question of another. The answer should come in the form of subtext, rather than dialogue.

Keep the thought of 'getting out early' in mind when it comes to redrafting your writing. Scan your scenes and see if you can heighten the drama by leaving words unsaid.

That was Our Exit!

Some themes come with inherent tension. Take divorce, death, moving house, personal injury or the loss of a job, for instance. Writing a scene around any of these matters has natural dramatic potential, putting characters under immense stress, and creating storylines with emotional highs and lows. But what if you could add a spoonful of stress to any scene, regardless of the theme?

Holding characters hostage by placing them in captive scenarios where they must endure something, or someone, in close proximity for an extended period can amp up stress and tension levels tenfold.

Write down names and brief character descriptions for two characters. They might be lovers, siblings, colleagues or flatmates, etc. Now decide on a fundamental issue or grievance, something which remains unresolved in their relationship. Perhaps they disagree on having children, buying a house, moving overseas, putting a parent into a retirement home, getting a puppy, buying or selling a caravan, or an important business decision.

Next, write a scene in which these two characters are driving cross-country to attend an event to which one of them does not want to go. This might be a wedding, funeral, conference, court case, convention, or otherwise. This is the surface level disagreement, and the confines of the car and the road trip simply provide a pressure-cooker environment for them to argue. Whether you decide that they run out of fuel, get lost, or end up driving the wrong way down a one-way street, have fun with subtext and expose the root of their fundamental grievance within the context of the scene.

Picture your characters, shoulder to shoulder in a car as they zoom down the motorway. Here are some subversive and provocative lines of dialogue to kick-start your imagination:

- I said we should have set off earlier.
- You said you knew the way.
- I assumed you'd know how to follow a map.
- Let's just stop for something to eat.
- Shall we just pull over and ask someone?
- I'm sure you've taken a wrong turn.
- The other route would have been much quicker.
- We should have gone by train.
- Great. We're lost.
- I can call my dad; he'll know.
- Can we just turn the music off for a while?
- Do you need some coffee?
- I said we should have filled up at the last petrol station.
- Do you have to have the window down?
- If you're tired, let's just pull over. I'll drive.

Don't underestimate the impact of an audience within the scene. Imagine, say, an arguing husband and wife arrive at the hospital bedside of his sick father, they may not feel able to continue their battle in front of other family members, but the issue at the heart of their disagreement remains unresolved. How would the scene play out?

Other potential 'captive scenarios' might include a journey by rail or air, a formal family dinner where everyone is expected to be on their best behaviour, a wedding ceremony where an argument on someone's happy day and in a place of worship would almost certainly be awkward for everyone.

THE ELEMENTS

She Turns and Walks Away

An easy way to create subtextual tension is by having a character express their thoughts and feelings through actions or gestures, as directed in the action of your screenplay, or stage directions in a play. For example:

                    SOFIA
        Are you okay, Mummy?

                    ANDREA
        I'm fine, darling. Really.

    SHE TURNS AWAY FROM THE CHILDREN, CRYING
    INTO HER APRON.

If you look at Arthur Miller's Death of a Salesman, *it's laced with this kind of direction which runs counter to the dialogue. Of course, for a fiction writer penning a romance novel in prose, which is intended to be read rather than performed, this technique is a given, and the 'show don't tell' rule is turned on its head:*

  '"Of course he's your baby," she said, looking away.'

Take a scene from your play or screenplay and highlight every time that a character answers a question directly. Now think about how you might replace their verbal answer with a silent action or gesture. Doing so will immediately replace text with subtext and leave your scene tighter and more engaging.

In practice, you may not want to do this in every scenario, but trying it out across a whole exchange or scene in your script will help you see the power at your fingertips.

Thematic Subtext

The theme of your play or screenplay is what holds it together, giving your story a reason (and a need!) to be told. Theme is the backdrop of your story and serves to express the values and messages that run deep within it, whilst underpinning what the story is really about. It is helpful to think of theme as the broader subtext of your script since it may not be directly stated. Great as your characters and their dialogue might be, without a strong theme, your writing will always feel like something is missing.

With my verbatim darma, In the Tall Grass, *I set Shade Schuler's murder in Dallas against the backdrop of the continuing transgender-murder epidemic across the United States and thus the theme is transgender empowerment, the urgent need for equality, and the marginalisation of a neglected section of society. In* The Importance of Being Earnest, *Oscar Wilde presents the seemingly impossible task of being genuine, sincere and earnest in a time when he viewed society as pompous and self-righteous. The subtext and theme: Victorian hypocrisy. In musical theatre too,* Kinky Boots *explores themes of conquering prejudice and surpassing stereotypes, whilst* Matilda *addresses bullying and a child's empowerment in various forms.*

Below are four different ways to establish strong thematic subtext in your work. Grab a marker pen and a stack of Post-it notes, and think about how each of these might apply to your script.

1. *Central question*: Think of the central theme of your script as the seed that it will grow from – the foundation that your writing is built upon. Whilst other elements of your script may alter and develop over time, the theme will be the one thing which likely won't change, so keep it clear in your mind before thinking about the structure, characters or anything else. As you get to know your characters and

craft their dialogue, these elements will shine a spotlight on your theme and inform how you ultimately present it to the audience. Define this central theme as a single word – e.g. love, money, hope, humanity, equality, faith, morality, survival and write it in big letters on a Post-it note.

2. *Moral question*: Can your theme be summed up in a single, moral question? – e.g. 'What is the real price of fame?', 'Is true love blind?' or 'Can money buy happiness?' Take another Post-it note, or join a few together and write your central question in big bold letters.

3. *Zeitgeist*: Are you able to tap into a thematic zeitgeist, either politically, socially or otherwise, to represent what's going on around us in the world today? Does your work address social acceptance, healthcare, interconnectivity, a national crisis or the state of the nation? If so, write it down on a Post-it note!

4. *Character*: Make use of your characters to show theme. Characters will likely make moral, physical or psychological choices during their journey – e.g. The way that your protagonist stops at nothing to bring down a terror organisation might speak to their feelings about justice, morality or retribution. For each character in your work, identify an overarching theme and write it on a Post-it note.

Now go ahead and stick your collection of Post-it notes on the wall in your writing space. Post-its relating to individual characters could be stuck next to a photo or picture which best represents them. You can read more about creating a story wall on page 161.

A Literary Bouquet

'From her fair and unpolluted flesh may violets spring!'

Hamlet, *William Shakespeare*

Flowers and literature have long been entwined. From In the
Garden of Eden *in George Bernard Shaw's* Back to Methuselah,
to the hidden splendour of Frances Hodgson Burnett's The
Secret Garden, *there is something beautiful and romantic about
a floral metaphor. In* A Midsummer Night's Dream,
*Shakespeare paints a vivid blanket of wildflowers in the scene
where Oberon, King of the Fairies, talks to his messenger Puck
about the spot where Queen Titania is sleeping…*

> I know a bank where the wild thyme blows,
> Where oxlips and the nodding violet grows,
> Quite over-canopied with luscious woodbine,
> With sweet musk-roses and with eglantine:
> There sleeps Titania sometime of the night,
> Lull'd in these flowers with dances and delight…

*Shakespeare also used flowers and plants to illustrate subtext. In
Hamlet, Ophelia expresses her feelings of sorrow and grief at the
murder of her father, Polonius, by handing flowers to the court.
Whilst most believe that the flowers are imagined in Ophelia's
delusional state of mind, some directors opt for literal flowers.
Either way, most agree that the flowers in the text have a specific
meaning and are not just a random assortment.*

*In the past, most flowers had their own vocabulary and held a
specific meaning. Whilst we may not be familiar with such
definitions today, we still give flowers as an expression of
endearment, or to provide comfort during hard times or in grief;
often we send flowers as subtext, to express the words that we
might feel unable to articulate directly – sympathy, thanks or
love…*

THE ELEMENTS

Look at your protagonist's story arc and pick out a single stand-out plot point – a significant moment in their journey when they reach an all-time low or a considerable high. Now, using the list of flower meanings below, craft a floral bouquet using flowers which seem fitting to the protagonist's current status. Next, write a short gift-card message to your protagonist, explaining why you are sending the bouquet, complete with your hopes and wishes, or a word or two of support or advice for the next stage of their journey.

Flower meanings

Amaryllis lily for pride and beauty
Anemone for forsakenness
Angelica for inspiration
Arum lily for faith and purity
Belladonna for silence
Bluebell for loyalty
Boronia for sweetness
Carnation (red) for divine love
Carnation (deep red) for a wounded heart
Carnation (striped) for refusal
Carnation (yellow) for disdain
Chrysanthemum (red) for love
Chrysanthemum (white) for truth
Chrysanthemum (yellow) for slighted love
Columbine for adultery
Cyclamen for diffidence
Daffodil for rebirth or renewal
Daisy for innocence
Fennel for flattery
Forget Me Not for everlasting love

Holly for festivity
Hyacinth (coloured) for playfulness
Hyacinth (white) for discretion
Hydrangea for cold-heartedness
Iris for wisdom
Jasmine for conviviality
Jonquil for hopefulness
Lavender for caution
Lilac for new love
Lily (white) for purity
Narcissus for narcissism
Nigella for uncertainty
Pansy for faithfulness or goodwill
Peony for bashfulness
Ranunculus for allure
Rose (china) for beauty
Rose (red) for love
Rose (white) for promise
Rose (yellow) for jealousy
Rosemary for remembrance
Rue for repentance

Sunflower (*dwarf*) for worship   *Tulip* (*red*) for love
Sunflower (*tall*) for pride   *Tulip* (*yellow*) for indifference
Sweet pea for wistfulness   *Violet* for fidelity
Sweet William for bravery   *Waterlily* for virtue
Tuberose for pleasure   *Zinnia* for memories

SUBTEXT

Why not inspire your writing week by taking your floral design to your local florist? Add a breath of fresh air to your writing space with your own living literary bouquet. I'd love to see your creation – why not share your arrangement with fellow writers online using the hashtag #LiteraryBouquet

SETTING

'Nothing can happen nowhere.
The locale of the happening always colours the happening,
and often, to a degree, shapes it.'

Elizabeth Bowen

This part of the book takes a look at setting: a fundamental element of any dramatic work which must be fully developed in order to establish a world and maintain continuity and credibility.

People exist in a particular time and place, so the setting of your script influences the way characters behave, it affects their dialogue, foreshadows events within the story, helps to set the mood and often invokes an emotional response. Get the setting right, and you lay firm foundations on which to write a great script.

Rain Later. Good, Occasionally Poor

Any dramatic script is comprised of two main parts: the lines of dialogue and the stage directions (or the action, in a screenplay). Stage directions are often the only place where writers for stage and screen have the opportunity to write prose as opposed to dialogue. Whilst it's fair and reasonable for us to keep this brief (remembering theatre is a collaborative art form, and we should try to avoid 'directing on the page'), opening stage directions, especially those which introduce a new location for the first time, are our opportunity to bring a place to life for the reader and in turn the audience. By doing so, we can ensure all who enter our world do so with a real sense of place and see the world precisely as we imagined it.

This exercise, inspired by the UK Met Office's Shipping Forecast,* will help you to escape your current setting and vividly visualise another. Once you have a clear picture of this place in your mind, we will look at how to turn it into a well-crafted opening stage direction. If you are reading this outside of the UK, you can listen to the Shipping Forecast online, and whilst it may at first sound like an incomprehensible stream of strange words and numbers, it is, in fact, a vital forecast for sailors and fishermen navigating the waters around the British Isles. It has also become somewhat of a national institution and a source of comfort for millions of radio listeners. I love it – the sound of strange far-off places with intriguing names (Viking, Forties, Dogger, Fisher), weather conditions that will only really mean anything to the brave souls sailing in them, and the relaxing melodic delivery of the announcer. It is all at once calming, yet brimming with dramatic potential and a touch of whimsy. It immediately evokes a strong sense of place, and for this reason, it is perfect for our purpose.

* The Shipping Forecast broadcasts on BBC Radio 4 four times each day. You can also stream previous broadcasts on demand from the BBC website. Each forecast is approximately nine minutes long. The 00:48 broadcast is extra special as it opens with 'Sailing By', a light piece of music composed by Ronald Binge, itself now synonymous with the forecast.

Listen to the Shipping Forecast and allow yourself to be transported to a distant land – wherever your imagination takes you. I like to sit in a comfy chair with just a small table lamp, or a candle flickering gently.

As you listen, what images come to mind? Can you visualise yourself in the scene, or are you an observer? Perhaps you are looking out to sea from the top of a lighthouse, watching out for lost ships at night, or maybe you are standing behind a railing on the seafront watching waves crash onto the rocks below?

In your notebook, write the words 'I SEE' in the middle of the page and start to brainstorm words around this that you associate with the picture in your mind. These can be descriptive of the setting, the mood evoked, general thoughts, feelings, your comfort level or merely associated words – e.g. stormy, gaslight, howling wind, uneasy, moonlight, trepidation, tea flask, radio static, fish, cold, loneliness… whatever you see, feel, think or sense.

Next, referring to your brainstorm, start to organise the words or phrases you have written into the following four categories, all of which are vital ingredients to help us write a great opening stage direction that is descriptive, not prescriptive. You can either highlight the words on your brainstorm in different colours or rewrite them in list form.

- *Fabric and texture of place*: The visual and physical properties which evoke emotions.

- *Light and colour*: The brightness, contrast and filter through which you see the location.

- *Soundscape*: Sounds, background or ambient noise which complement the visual.

- *Mood and tone*: The atmosphere of the place and any feelings you have towards it.

Feel free to disregard any miscellaneous words that don't fit easily into these categories at this stage. Look at the words you have placed in each category. Does one word stand out from the rest? Pick a single word from each category which you feel summarises the texture, light, mood and sound of your location and use these to write an opening stage direction which immediately transports your reader to the scene.

Whilst the opening stage direction for Arthur Miller's *Death of a Salesman* fills the whole page of the script, leaving little to the imagination, in *Waiting for Godot*, Samuel Beckett gives us simply, '*A Country Road. A Tree. Evening.*' Personally, I like to aim for something in the middle, giving enough information to portray a sense of place on the page, then allowing the cast and creative team to bring that place to life. Don't be afraid to take your time in 'painting' an important location in vivid colour. Good scene descriptions make a script easier for the reader to visualise and the audience to experience.

The City and Sex

'New York City is all about sex. People getting it, people trying to get it, people who can't get it. No wonder the city never sleeps. It's too busy trying to get laid.'

Sex and the City

Manhattan was arguably the fifth character in Sex and the City, *the romantic comedy-drama television series created by Darren Star from Candace Bushnell's book, which ran from 1998 to 2004. Carrie Bradshaw, head of the quartet of single women, declared in one episode that when she first moved to New York City, she often bought* Vogue *instead of dinner, stating, 'I just felt it fed me more.' When she wasn't strutting along Fifth Avenue in the latest pair of Manolo Blahniks, or stepping out for the star-studded opening of a new Asian-fusion eatery in the Meatpacking District, Bradshaw was burning the midnight oil in her cosy brownstone apartment, penning her latest column for the fictional newspaper,* The New York Star. *Manhattan is woven into the fabric of the show in such a fundamental way – just try and transplant the girls and their stories to, say… Abu Dhabi? (For that, there's the spin-off film* Sex and the City 2.)

So why was Manhattan so important to the show? Well, not only did it provide a well-known backdrop in terms of the actual setting, but it gave the writing team NYC-centric storylines and cultural themes, which boiled down to a distinct 'voice' for the show, not forgetting localised dialect, language and attitude.

By evoking a strong sense of place, you can help your audience connect with the world with which you are presenting them, and buy into your story. If you have direct experience of a place, that's great. If not, check out Exercise 4.3: Visiting a Soul Place *on page 169. You might also seek out resources such as films, photographs, local newspapers, artwork, music and social history.*

Once you have a good sense of place in your mind, whether through personal experience or collected research, we are going to use our five senses (sight, sound, smell, touch and taste) to transport our audience into the world we are creating. It's easy to give in to visual descriptions, but there is so much more.

Write a short scene with a generic setting (a café, family home, library, supermarket) in which two characters never mention their location, but through use of sensory detail, we know where your scene is set. Here are some tips for tuning into each of the senses:

• *What does it look like in your world?*

Try to look beyond generic blue skies and green trees – light and weather are often unique to a place. When I moved from London to Texas in 2015, I was immediately aware of the different hues in the sky, the position of the sun throughout the day, the constellations of stars I had never seen before… probably due to London smog and light pollution! Paint vivid pictures in both your dialogue and stage directions or action. If I ask you to think up a snapshot image of communist North Korea and socialist South Korea… the colour palettes you will visualise for each will be vastly different. Referencing desaturated colours verses a bright and vivid landscape will evoke a strong sense of place. Use these tones to colour your dialogue too, with characters speaking from a world of freedom, charisma and optimism in contrast to a place that might be dull, subdued, guarded and utilitarian.

• *What does it sound like in your world?*

Does your world have any distinctive dialogue? Writing accurate patterns of speech and using local dialect words, terms of endearment, elisions, colloquialisms and expletives will all build towards a unique sense of place. However, do take care not to alienate your audience or your readers – go easy with the use of unfamiliar words and phrases with obscure meanings. If your scene plays out by the coast, how can you capture the screeching of gulls or the blast of a ship's horn and convey this in your work? Achieving a sense of interior and exterior sound on the page will transport readers to the beating heart of your story. Find unique ways to write the 'white noise' of inner-city living or nature's song in the wilderness, likewise the eerie echoes of hospital corridors or the creaking doors and floors of an historic home.

- *What does it smell like in your world?*

  Smells usually evoke one of two reactions: aversion or attraction. Does your character cover their nose to escape the smell of soot from a London Underground or Manhattan subway platform during their daily commute? Do they know they are home with the first smell of salty sea air through the coach window? Or perhaps they are returning to their childhood home in Louisiana to the spicy aroma of a neighbourhood crawfish boil?

- *What does it feel like in your world?*

  Does a warm Pacific Ocean breeze enhance an LA love scene? Or can a cosy autumn night in the Outer Hebrides warm hearts in the Highlands? Think about atmosphere too. Television crime dramas are great at evoking a sense of unease and tension through 'feelings' offered up by their settings. Think of the blustery scenes on the Dorset coastline in *Broadchurch*, or the eerily dark tones of *Top of the Lake*, shot entirely on location on New Zealand's South Island. At a micro-level, can the touch of a sticky vinyl tablecloth transport you to a greasy East End caff? Imagine the slippery rocks of the Giant's Causeway, the warm sands of a Goan beach and the battering winds of Boston, and utilise them in dialogue and directions.

- *What does it taste like in your world?*

  Clichéd as it may be, there is a reason why so many movies and TV shows have cops eating doughnuts and sipping coffee. It immediately evokes the sense of a busy US metropolis, feeling that at any moment a call over the radio will see them thrust into action. Try to push further and think of the 'taste' of an actual location – think about the dry mouth you get whilst driving down a dirt track in the summer, or the 'taste' of diesel whilst filling up at the gas station. What about the damp, musty air of an abandoned building or a caravan or holiday home that has stood empty? Not forgetting the taste of a sweet fairground kiss or the unsavoury lick of affection from a passionate pooch!

When the senses combine, you can enhance your writing and draw your audience into your work, either directly through dialogue, subversively in the subtext, or as prose in your action or stage directions. Remembering that your script is at some point going to become a blueprint for a director and cast to work from, if the locale is essential to the world of your play or screenplay, you should utilise sensory detail to weave it into the fabric of your work.

The Dentist's Chair... on Mars

Sometimes when you have an idea for a new script, the setting is determined by the plot. If you are writing a crime thriller in which the LAPD reopens the cold case of a Venice Beach slaying or a political drama about whistleblowing in Westminster... then you're probably good to go. But what about that human story you have in mind, where the mother/daughter relationship is front and centre, and the locale doesn't come to mind straight away?

Deciding on the right setting for your work is an important decision. The location you choose can help to steer the plot, add tone, mood and atmosphere, and supply tension and conflict. It can also provide a plethora of options for writing location-centric subplots and good backstories.

If you have an idea but no location in mind already, hold that thought. If not, for the sake of this exercise, jot down a quick non-descript idea for a dramatic scene; for example, two brothers return to their family home after school to find the house is empty and their parents have left without a trace. Or a vulnerable elderly woman reclines in the dentist chair of her son, whom she doesn't know is a serial killer. With a large inheritance awaiting him... how much anaesthetic is too much?

Next, along the top of a blank page, write five possible locations where the scene could play out. Try to think outside the box. If your story is generic, how can you make it unique? What if the dangerous dentist's chair was, say... on Mars? Now, under each location idea, list the factors relating to each location which might add to the scene. Consider each location's unique offering including the light (or lack of), weather conditions, neighbours, the language spoken, the remoteness... anything else you can think of. Here is a list of intriguing reasons why I might consider setting my killer-dentist scene on Mars:

- It's way below-freezing.

- Gravity on Mars is less than that on Earth – bags of comic potential with the chair alone.

- Since I'm writing in the sci-fi genre, it can be as desolate or densely populated as I decide.

- Potential for fun dialect exploration when scripting Martians.

- If the anaesthetic doesn't kill, there's always boiling blood and radiation!

- An unexplored terrain to excite the senses (see *Exercise 3.4.2: The City and Sex* on page 117).

Now review your current work in progress and check that you have exploited the location for all it has to offer. Always question your choice of setting and ask yourself, 'Why does my story have to be told here?' Or 'Could this story take place somewhere with more significant dramatic/comic/tragic effect?'

Perspective of Place

We all see and experience things and places differently. When thinking about your setting and writing dialogue relating to or driven by your locale, consider the different perspectives of the characters in your scenes.

For example, a single parent struggling to put food on the table is likely to view the aisles of a supermarket very differently than his wealthy neighbour. Could a scene set in the canned-food aisle be emotionally tense and spark conflict when the two characters meet? With these characters in mind, imagine a scene where the subtext of an argument over parking on their shared driveway is wealth, jealousy and judgement? A war veteran, who has lost a limb in the line of duty, and his carefree twin brother will both experience different emotions on a family beach holiday. The subtext of the ex-military brother's reluctance to swim is limitless. But in both scenarios, the choice of setting is used to drive the emotions and conflict in the scenes.

Expand your thinking about the perspective of place by coming up with a scene idea set in the following locations. As with the examples above, your scene should involve two characters, a source of conflict and subtext. With each location, consider personal points of view, emotional states and judgements. How does each character feel about the place and what emotions are triggered?

- A crowded airport departure lounge.

- An after-hours hospital waiting room.

- A noisy children's soft-play centre.

- The quiet coach on a train.

- The swim-up bar in a resort hotel.

This exercise will help you to add depth to your settings that reflect both your characters and the world around them. It will also help you to choose locations based on their dramatic potential, or to seek it out in the ones you've already selected.

Beats Keats

John Keats once said, 'My imagination is a monastery, and I am its monk.' In this exercise, I implore you to be your best monk and enjoy every untold corner of your monastery.

The wonderful thing about poetry, more than any other form of creative writing, is that there really are no rules. Beauty is in the eye of the beholder, words are in the pen of the creator, and everything is subjective. Take structure, form, shape and everything that has ever felt restrictive – and throw them out of the window. Rip up the rule book. Inspiration is all around us, so let's harness it without limitation and write something beautiful. In fact… words are all around us: in instruction manuals, takeaway menus, messages scribbled on the walls of public toilets, labels on bottles of ketchup… literally everywhere!

I have adapted this exercise from the practice of 'found poetry' (taking words, phrases, and sometimes whole passages from other sources and reframing them), in this instance approaching the convention in the form of a scavenger hunt. I love exercises like this one that get us out of the house and away from our desks, offering fresh air whilst still being productive.

Simply grab a notebook and head outdoors. Seek out any written words that you might see, however unrelated or mundane they may seem, which we will curate into a page of literary beauty.

- If you are on holiday or live by the coast, talk a walk along the beach. You might find words on washed-up artefacts, scraps of litter or on newspaper pages.

- Take a stroll through woodland, looking for love letters or initials carved into trees, plaques on benches, interesting branches or twigs that resemble letters, signposts or tourist-information boards.

- On your daily commute to work, note down advertisements on bus stops, unusual business names or destinations, and graffiti on the back of the seat in front of you.

- Walk along your own street and notice any street signs, personalised car registration plates, council notices, roadwork signs or parking information.

- In your own home, rifle through your medicine box and note down dosage instructions, look at the ingredients on a can of baked beans, read junk mail looking for any interesting names or words, write down instructions from the instruction manual of your waffle maker or note items found on your shopping list.

Once you have filled a page in your notebook with some interesting words or phrases, let's look at some potential themes for your poem. You should approach this next step much the same way you would when making a collage or scrapbook. How can you best arrange your source material to create the most pleasing or satisfying poem? Well, having a theme in mind will help. Here are some ideas…

- Your first love/days in the sun.

- Bereavement/memories of a loved one.

- Childhood memories/your happy place.

- Future goals/your grand plan/dreams.

Whatever your theme, having it in mind as you look through your notes and the exciting objects that you have collected will help you to see them with new meaning. Remember, your source material is just a starting point. Feel free to add and remove words and mould it to serve your purpose. It is there to inspire not restrict you. Your poem might be funny, moving or enlightening… but it is sure to be 100% unique.

Here is a quick example of a poem that I was inspired to write using words I collected whilst walking my dogs:

In memory of Eileen George, who loved this park and view,
Caution: hidden cables outside number twenty-two.
Bins go out on Thursdays, inform the city council,
No circulars! No junk mail! The Pohutukawa trees,
    delightful.
'Nine cases of measles!' The Herald has confided,
Please pick up after your dogs, and use the bins provided!

Try this exercise whilst on a visit to a location that relates with
your current project. See *Exercise 4.3: Visiting a Soul Place* on
page 169.

PLOT

'What makes a good plot? A high concept? An idea you can pitch in twenty-five words? Something zeitgeisty? Aliens? Ghosts? Royalty? Marriage? Maybe. Maybe not. What makes a good plot is a plot you can bear to live with. A plot you love. A plot that will feed your soul.'

Phil Hughes

Put simply, plot is the series of events which provide conflict within a story. The spine of any story, a plot should be easy to communicate without need to mention specific character names or places. See *Exercise 6.4: The Logline Test* on page 198.

Great plays and films have great plots, with the power to captivate audiences and evoke any number of emotions. Of course, they all start with a great script with a beginning, middle and end… plus some unexpected twists and turns along the way. The exercises in this part will help you to write more dynamic exposition and explore your characters' story arcs, whilst offering tips and tricks to crank up the drama and raise the stakes a little too.

Notes on Dramatic Structure

Plays first originated in Ancient Greece. Aristotle was one of the first to write about drama, and described it as having three parts: a beginning, a middle and an end. Further developed by Roman poets and playwrights, these parts were later called Protasis, Epitasis and Catastrophe. As drama evolved over the centuries, other dramatists expanded on Aristotle's theory and argued that dramatic structure could more accurately be divided up into five acts.

In the 1800s, German playwright Gustav Freytag plotted the dramatic arc of the five-act structure as he defined it, in what has become known as Freytag's Pyramid. This diagram is still commonly used today when we talk about plot structure and can be tracked in most plays, movies and television dramas. It is also used to analyse classical theatre, including Shakespeare's plays.

The diagram below places Freytag's Pyramid on top of Aristotle's three-act structure and the five-act structure developed by the Romans.

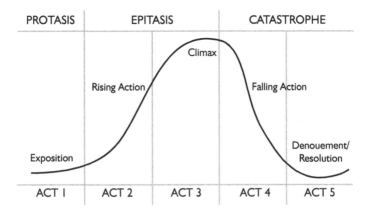

The plot points of the five-act structure are as follows:

- *Act 1 – The Exposition* is the beginning of the story, where the audience learns about the characters and the setting.

- *Act 2 – Rising Action* is where actions or events lead towards the central conflict, and ultimately, towards the height of the problem. Complications arise for the protagonist.

- *Act 3 – The Climax* is the pinnacle of the story. Everything hits the fan. This is the point of no return for the protagonist when everything changes.

- *Act 4 – Falling Action* is when all of the pieces of the puzzle begin to fall into place and where unknown details or plot twists are revealed and wrapped up.

- *Act 5 – Denouement* or *Resolution* is the final outcome. The protagonist has won or lost, the battle is over and usually a moral or lesson is learned.

Considered the earliest surviving work of dramatic theory, Aristotle's *Poetics* is the foundation of drama as we know it. However, for today's reader, the language and ideas are somewhat obtuse and can be hard to decipher. For help unpacking many of Aristotle's theories (and a wonderful education on playwriting in general), Stephen Jeffreys' book, *Playwriting* (Nick Hern Books, 2019) is essential reading.

Invisible Exposition

Exposition can be a necessary evil of storytelling. Too much, and you risk holding back a story like the string on a helium balloon – starving the audience of drama and conflict and subjecting them to the 'history' on the world of the play/screenplay. Not enough exposition, and you deprive your audience of the vital information they need to know and understand in order for character arcs and plot points to make sense. Good exposition requires a delicate balance, requiring the writer to convey nuggets of information seamlessly, as and when required, without losing momentum or believability.

Here are some pitfalls to avoid and some pointers to keep in mind as you master invisible exposition:

Pitfalls

- *Avoid having characters share or receive essential information by hearing things on the radio or television, or reading letters, email and text messages aloud to themselves.*

- *Try to steer clear of dream sequences, flashbacks and extended prologues. It might work in an established serial drama, but can read as lazy in a spec script.*

- *If it's not pivotal to the story, plot or character arcs, you probably don't need it. Always avoid dumbing down – the audience needs to be challenged with a certain degree of 'decoding' in order to stay interested. By all means, flesh out your characters' backstories thoroughly, but do so in a separate document… and leave it there.*

- *Remember that an audience that has questions is an audience that is invested. And therein lies the answer of how to keep an audience hooked until the end. You don't need to answer every question, so try to avoid the temptation.*

Pointers

- *Use exposition to build or break tension, thus enhancing a scene rather than detracting from it. Far better to back your character into a corner and force them to reveal information within an emotional or dramatic scene, than offering it up. If the facts to convey are potentially bland, there should be a good reason why they are sharing them – something must be at stake.*

- *Keep it brief! When exposition is spread thinly, you will find it easier to weave into the narrative of your script. Use exposition to strengthen existing character arcs as turning points, reveals, plants and pay-offs. Interrupting the story flow will almost certainly read as too 'on the nose'.*

- *Have characters argue or react differently to shared information, using exposition to draw conflict and/or comic potential. If you ever watched the American sitcom* Friends, *remember all we learned about Ross and Monica's childhood. Yes, there were a lot of flashback scenes, but at other times a disagreement would spark a reveal of information from their past, defining their characters to great comic effect.*

Read the following scene.

```
SHARON VISITS STEVE. SHE KNOCKS ONCE
BEFORE ENTERING HIS APARTMENT WHERE SHE
IS MET BY THE STALE SMELL OF DESPONDENCY
AND OLD TAKEAWAY CONTAINERS. SHE OBSERVES
AN UNKEMPT STEVE, SLUMPED IN FRONT OF A
HOME-SHOPPING CHANNEL.

                SHARON
   Shall I open the curtains, Steve?
   It's a lovely day outside.
```

This example could easily have been a scene in which Steve explains to Sharon how depressed he is feeling since losing his job. Instead, his unkempt appearance and disorderly living room tells the same story, cutting straight to a line of dialogue which advances the plot.

Write an opening stage direction, followed by a line or two of dialogue for one of the following scenarios. How can you make use of visual storytelling to *show* instead of telling?

Scenarios

- Heidi returns to the house she once shared with Richard to collect the last of her things, following a very public divorce.

- Tyler is not happy to see his ex-prison friend, Ken, who turns up at the coffee shop where he now works.

- Bram has a history of financial problems. His girlfriend Keisha is wary when he applies for a credit card in her name.

A quick reminder…

- *Good exposition:*
    - Invisible.
    - Information is extracted or revealed organically.
- *Bad exposition:*
    - Too much backstory.
    - Everything is 'on the nose'.
    - Information is offered.

Pick a Path

What if your protagonist doesn't open the cellar door and stumble upon the entrance to a lost kingdom? What if the twins are never reunited? What if the demons who possess the old lady can't be exorcised, and her only escape is death? What if…?

Before we were all crushing candy on tiny screens or lost in the virtual reality of 3D video games, as children we got our adventure fix from books. The magical days of getting lost in the rabbit warren of a 'choose your own adventure' or 'pick a path' book meant hours of excitement lay in wait at the turn of each page. You, the reader, were in charge of your own destiny. Should you climb the ladder and battle the evil warlock? Or stumble through the enchanted orchard in search of the lost chalice?

If you are getting stuck with plot development, try sprinkling some of the magic those clever children's fantasy writers used and see if you can unlock a door to something special.

You can use this exercise to help you plot out the basic structure of a new play or screenplay, or, if you are working on a project that has lost its way, maybe considering an alternative path for your protagonist will put a spring in their step and propel them on a different or more exciting journey.

The chart on the next page incorporates the five elements of plot: exposition, rising action, climax, falling action and denouement (resolution), as prescribed in Freytag's Pyramid (see *Notes on Dramatic Structure* on page 129–31), with additional choices, so that you may consider a total of four potential plotlines with four different endings. Start off by copying the chart onto a large sheet paper, leaving the boxes empty.

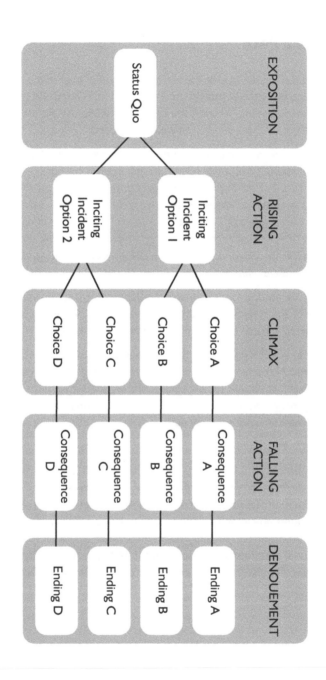

Next, think about the world of your script as it exists beyond the window of time within which we view it. Decide upon the moment in which we enter the story and meet your protagonist. You should ask yourself, 'Why now?' Does the entry point have sufficient dramatic potential? If not, would it be better to meet your protagonist at a different point in time? Perhaps at a crossroads in their life, or after a major low or just before a significant high? Once you have this, note it down in the exposition box.

Great! You've got your jumping-off point. *Now the fun bit…* Something must happen to upset the apple cart. An inciting incident must unbalance the protagonist's world and change the status quo, introducing the question at the heart of your script (see the next exercise, *Did You Lock the Door?*). But what? Think of two possible options here and note them down on the chart. As you fine-tune your structure in more detail later (using Syd Field's paradigm if writing a screenplay – see page 168), a turning point will precede the climax, further raising the stakes and reframing the central question. But for now, and for simplicity, allow yourself the freedom to dream up two possible climaxes for each of your inciting incidents. Next, jot down the fallout from each of these in the falling action boxes. Finally, dream up four possible endings, each should be different based on the choices that your protagonist made during the earlier stages of the story arc.

Considering different paths for your protagonist – different outcomes, consequences and possible pay-offs – is what makes your job as a writer so exciting and liberating. Tiny changes at the beginning can have fundamental effects further down the path. See *Exercise 4.2: Post-it Plotlines* on page 166 for an exercise in experimenting with sequence and structure.

THE ELEMENTS

Did You Lock the Door?

In the teaching of screenwriting structure, specifically when looking at 'turning points', you may hear about the idea of the 'inciting incident', sometimes referred to as a 'disturbance' – the idea that something must happen relatively early on in your story which upsets or disturbs the status quo; the point from which there is no going back for your protagonist. It is helpful to think of this as the first in a series of closing doors that your protagonist will pass through.

The 'something' which pushes your protagonist through the first door might materialise in the form of a devastating piece of news, a sudden death or life-altering accident, the arrival of something or someone from the past, the revealing of a secret, or anything else that might present a threat or challenge to their world and the status quo. How they respond to this, and the subsequent journey they must go on as a result, may then force them to go through further closing doors as they seek to fix things and re-establish equilibrium.

For instance, if your character crashes their car into a convenience store in the middle of the night, setting off the security alarm and alerting the police, this has forced your protagonist through a doorway from which there is no going back. They have committed a driving offence and must deal with the fallout. However, if your protagonist then decides to drive away instead of waiting for the police to arrive, this decision has forced them through a second door which slams shut behind them. Put simply, your protagonist makes an irrevocable decision, prompting whatever sequence of events that follows.

The American crime comedy-drama television series Good Girls is an excellent example of this. A series of questionable decisions force the three friends through door after door of high-stakes drama where turning back is never an option.

To write good turning points, you first need to be able to identify them. For this practical exercise, rewatch your favourite movie with a notebook in hand and look out for disturbances in the story – what are the 'doorways of no return'?

There are two crucial elements to look out for and understand. Firstly, what is the event, factor or force, that propels the protagonist through the doorway? – e.g. crashing into a convenience store. Secondly, what is the thing that locks the door firmly behind them, taking the option of turning around and going home off the table? – e.g. fleeing the scene.

With this structural device clear in your mind, consider if there might be scope to make life a little harder for your protagonist in order to raise the stakes, thus increasing the drama. Are both elements described above present in your work? Are you sure you locked the door?

The Six-Million-Dollar Story

In 1995, American writer Kurt Vonnegut gave a lecture in which he spoke about the thesis for his master's degree, explaining, 'There's no reason why the simple shapes of stories can't be fed into computers,' he said. 'They are beautiful shapes.' His thesis may have been rejected by the University of Chicago, but Vonnegut was clearly on to something. In 2016, researchers from the Computational Story Lab at Burlington's University of Vermont picked up the baton that Vonnegut had thrown down, and proceeded to data-mine over 1,700 works of fiction, discovering that they all followed one of six emotional arcs.

You can still enjoy Vonnegut's entertaining lecture on YouTube. In it, he draws a graph showing what he calls the G/I Axis (Good fortune vs. Ill fortune) to demonstrate simple story structures. He begins with the recognisable 'Man in a Hole' arc – 'man falls into hole, man gets out of hole', followed by 'Boy meets Girl' – 'boy meets girl, boy loses girl, boy gets girl.' Finally, the million-dollar 'Cinderella story' structure – '[It's] the most popular story in our Western civilization. Every time it's retold somebody makes another million dollars. You're welcome to do it.'

The 2016 study isn't intended to restrict us writers to a finite number of plots – Aristotle was trying to categorise stories by type over two thousand years before Vonnegut and the Vermont researchers – their analysis simply highlights the existence of six primary emotional arcs: 'We find a set of six core trajectories which form the building blocks of complex narratives.'

If you're looking for a tried-and-tested starting point, this exercise harnesses the power of six to generate an original story idea… *possibly even a million-dollar story!* Start by rolling a dice to select one of the six story structures from the list below, based on the Vermont University story-arc research:

1. *Rags to riches*: A steady rise from bad to good fortune.

2. *Riches to rags*: A fall from good to bad, a tragedy.

3. *Icarus*: A rise then a fall in fortune.

4. *Oedipus*: A fall, a rise then a fall again.

5. *Cinderella*: A rise, a fall, then a rise.

6. *Man in a hole*: A fall, then a rise.

PLOT

Next, roll the dice six more times to select other elements from the lists below:

Protagonist

1. Taxi driver
2. Nurse
3. President
4. Teacher
5. Baker
6. Doctor

Obstacle

1. Financial
2 Love
3. Loss
4. A secret
5. Self-confidence
6. Fear

Side-kick

1. Plumber
2. Mechanic
3. Writer
4. Witch
5. Yogi
6. Animal

Goal

1. Fortune/Security
2. Healing/Health
3. Love/Family
4. Escape/Survival
5. Reveal/Retrieve
6. Revenge/Destroy

First location

1. Bank
2. Coffee shop
3. Luxury yacht
4. Caravan
5. Jail cell
6. Funeral

Genre

1. Romance
2. Action
3. Historical
4. Thriller
5. Comedy
6. Fantasy

Use the story elements you have randomly generated as a starting point to write a scene or short story. Interpret the story elements however you wish, in a way that best serves the story you want to tell and your own writing style.

Baked to Plotfection

Just like a good cake, a good plot will often have more than one layer. In soap opera, the storyline document for each episode prescribes different storylines or story strands, listed as A, B and C (sometimes, more). An 'A story' is the main storyline, dominating the episode with the most number of scenes and as such is the primary focus of the episode. It best describes what the episode is about and dictates the central theme – the headline-grabbing stories that usually run across a whole week, month or even longer. A 'B story' will often run parallel to the A storyline, and whilst taking up less screen time, it will be the story stand that has the most impact on the A story, usually adding additional conflict and impacting the structural shape of the episode. These storylines have shorter story arcs and might only run across a few episodes. Finally, a 'C story' will generally be used for either a stand-alone or throw-away comedy scene (though crucially adding light relief and contrast to stories A and B) or to build a longer-term storyline slowly that will eventually become an A story. This is sometimes referred to as a 'runner' and will often only make up one or two scenes in a thirty-minute episode but should still have a set-up and a resolution of its own.

To use a very general and recognisable reference, in any given episode of the British version of The Office, *the character of David Brent usually gets the A story, whilst Tim and Dawn would provide the B story, and Gareth would be the C story.*

In this exercise, we'll look at adding layers to your plots by making the lives of your characters as multi-layered and three-dimensional as our own.

Start by thinking of your own life as though it were the plot of a TV soap opera… *or sit-com if the case may be!* Chances are you have more than one thing going on in your life at any given moment. You may have a primary focus or a current goal, but I'm guessing there are other things in the background, bubbling away on the back-burner of differing size, scale and scope? Maybe you have a current goal – e.g. to pass your driving test, or to finish your studies and graduate from university. Likely, you may also have long-term goals, like getting your foot on the property ladder, or getting married and starting a family. Then there are even longer-term goals, such as buying a holiday home, seeing your children go to university or your retirement plans.

Next, watch an episode of a TV soap opera. It doesn't matter if you are not a regular viewer and don't know the characters or their current storylines. Try to identify the different story strands in the episode, marking them down in your notebook as A, B and C as differentiated above. Note how they each interact and cross over to get the best out of each other and work as a complete script. As well as individual apartments and family homes, soap operas use 'communal sets', such as pubs, cafés, restaurants and launderettes, allowing characters to cross over in public locations and their varying storylines to dovetail seamlessly into one another.

Look for layers in your own work. Begin by brainstorming the A, B and C storylines in your script and identifying how they can best work together to enrich, highlight and contrast with each other to enhance your story. Think about what the goals are in their story arc in a way that makes sense to your script. What is the protagonist's current objective? How does this fit into their bigger plan? If or when they achieve it, what's next?

Change of Fortune

What's a writer to do whilst dining alone in a Chinese noodle bar? Well, I like to make use of the abundant fortune cookies and write short scenes inspired by the mysterious messages inside.

First, think up a quick on-the-spot character, someone who could use a change of fortune. No need to write this down, just off the top of your head, give them a name and a goal and an obstacle (conflict). *For example:*

- Simone – Wants to drive a taxi but has failed her driving test three times.

- Gary – Wants to grow his dairy business, but alternative milk products are trending.

- Blue – Wants to buy their own home but can't get on the property ladder.

Next, write a short scene (maybe four or five lines of dialogue) between your character and someone else in their world (friend/relative/co-worker, etc.) which shows their status quo and introduces the conflict. Now open the fortune cookie and use the message inside to write a second scene, showing how the change of fortune affects them. Finally, write a third scene which shows the resolution.

Give it a go! Next time you are waiting for your order or visit your favourite Chinese restaurant, ask for a fortune cookie. You can also pick up a multipack at your local Asian supermarket and keep one or two in your bag for when inspiration (or hunger) strikes!

145

The Ticking Time-Bomb

A ticking time-bomb, or a hard deadline, is a great way to put pressure on your characters and increase drama by adding suspense. We see it time and time again, most obviously in movies. The college football player who must lose his virginity by prom night, anyone? How about Cinderella? Be home before the clock strikes midnight, or else! Christmas movies, by definition, exploit the expectation of a perfect Christmas morning, using potentially devastated children to tug at our heartstrings. Santa must find the lost sleigh by Christmas Eve, to save Christmas for children around the world. Simple, right?!

Well, the reason all of these examples work is because the audience is aware of the situation and therefore emotionally invests in the race against time. Imagine if we were kept in the dark about the magical spell cast upon Cinderella by her Fairy Godmother, until the moment her carriage turned back into a pumpkin and her horses into mice: we would certainly still be surprised, but there would not have been any tension or emotional investment. That fact that we know about the hard deadline of midnight provides suspense.

> 'Four people are sitting around a table, talking about baseball. Five minutes of it, very dull. Suddenly a bomb goes off, blows the people to smithereens. What does the audience have? Ten seconds of shock. Now take the same scene. Tell the audience there is a bomb under the table and it will go off in five minutes. Well, the emotion of the audience is very different. Now the conversation about baseball becomes very vital because the audience is saying: "Don't be ridiculous. Stop talking about baseball, there's a bomb under there." You've got the audience working.'

This quote from Alfred Hitchcock teaches us that whilst shock and surprise are fleeting, suspense lasts. And here's the real shock... are you ready? Hitchcock followed his famous 'ticking time-bomb' discussion by saying, 'The bomb must never go off.' Sure, it's a race against time, but time, for your protagonist, must never run out... 'If you do this, then you've worked that audience into a state and they will be angry if you don't provide them with some relief.' *Of course, long before Hitchcock became known as the 'Master of Suspense', Aristotle had identified the dramatic unity of story, space and time, noting that tension was increased when time was restricted.*

Hollywood clichés of the frantic hero dripping sweat over a spaghetti of coloured wires, as the aeroplane plummets to the ground and the blinking red numbers countdown to zero are all best left in action movies. But let's look at some great tricks and devices that you can leverage to add suspense to your writing, with a metaphorical ticking time-bomb.

Identify areas in your script where adding a burden of time would put pressure on your characters. If you're not writing an action or adventure piece, think of everyday, naturalistic things. For example, Anna has decided that she does love Josie, so she rushes to the airport to persuade her not to take the new job in Canada, and to stay in Seattle and marry her instead. You might crank up the pressure even more by adding heavy traffic as Anna rushes to the airport, followed by lengthy airport security checks intercut with early boarding at the gate, etc. Other examples of 'time pressure' might include an eviction notice, a race against sunset, or a dwindling supply of food or water for a vulnerable character lost in the forest.

Next, make sure that the stakes are high enough to make the countdown matter. If Josie could just travel back to Seattle at weekends then maybe she and Anna could make a long-distance relationship work? Hmmm... that's a problem. Okay, Josie's new job had better be in the Rockies, somewhere with only one scheduled flight every month, totally off-the-grid, meaning video calls are not a viable option either. Better still, what if Josie's ex-girlfriend lives in the remote Canadian town she's heading for? Now the stakes are really high for Anna.

The possibilities are endless and are not restricted by genre. What about an impending pregnancy? In a matter of months/weeks/days there will be no hiding who the father is. A birthday? If your character robs the post office tomorrow he'll be sixteen and could go to jail; he must do it tonight when he can be prosecuted as a minor if he's caught. How about a terminal illness and a bucket list with an impossible list of items still to check off? Or what about a prison break? There is only a tiny window of opportunity whilst the guards switch over, or the laundry cart blocks the view of the CCTV camera.

Short time + tall orders = high stakes and serious suspense!

It's your job to make your characters' lives difficult… *seize the power at your fingertips.*

Six-Word Stories

Time is money! Nowhere is this more true than in screen and stage production. If a script reader in a literary department picks up your script, and two or three pages go by where nothing really happens, chances are they'll toss it aside and pick another one up. The first few pages really count, and in fact, many festivals or scriptwriting competitions now request that you only submit the first ten pages of your work. Every second of screen time costs a lot of money, so nobody is going to shoot a scene which doesn't move the story forward or add value to the storytelling in some way. If a painfully slow play or film does make it into production, it's highly likely that such scenes will later be cut in the rehearsal room or in the edit suite.

In the spirit of 'flash fiction', this exercise is designed to realise the potential of every word, by writing micro-stories. If you're the kind of person who throws a tube of toothpaste away once it gets close to the end, this exercise will force you to squeeze every last bit out. After all, that last bit wasn't free!

Legend has it that whilst lunching with friends, Ernest Hemingway made a bet that he could write an entire story in just six words, before penning the following on a napkin…

'For sale: baby shoes, never worn.'

Though Hemingway's authorship of this remains unsubstantiated, the six-word-story movement has taken hold. Stories certainly don't get much more economical!

Have a go at writing your own six-word story. If you're looking for some more inspiration, check out www.sixwordstories.net for some great examples. Here are three of my own…

• Fist clenched, anger released. Guilt? Forever.

- Wings clipped, his dreams became memories.

- She wanted him. He wanted him.

Since discovering the six-word-story movement, I try to write one every day on my typewriter as soon as I walk into my writing room. I find them a great way to warm up before a writing session, and since you can also quickly type these up on your phone, they are a creative way to pass the time when travelling.

Often, I find I want to know more about the characters and worlds the stories conjure up, so I'll use them as a writing prompt, either riffing off one for a freewriting session (see page 14) or using one to inspire a longer piece of work. Share your creations on Twitter with the hashtag #SixWordStories

#Awkward

Some of the best scenes in movies, TV dramas and plays come when characters are backed into corners, wrenched from their comfort zones, and put in awkward situations. Awkwardness = tension, so writing an awkward scene is a great way to inject a mixture of excitement, comedy, suspense and conflict into your writing. Embarrassing and uneasy situations are not reserved for cringe comedy shows like The Comeback, It's Always Sunny in Philadelphia *or* Curb Your Enthusiasm, *where the social awkwardness of the protagonists makes the audience squirm or reach for a cushion to hide behind. Dramatic and tragic scenes can also be heightened by adding a dose of discomfort. Imagine a scene at a dinner party where two couples are discussing the best ways to get pregnant, forgetting the third couple at the end of the table who may have experienced fertility problems, or even suffered the loss an infant.*

Here are four effective ways to make your scenes uncomfortable:

1. Adding a character: *Often, by simply adding a 'gooseberry' character into a scene, you can dial the cringe factor up to maximum: Noah and Tom are discussing an STD crisis whilst waiting for the doctor to return with their results. Why not plant a prudish pensioner in the waiting room?*

2. Switching locations: *Instead of having Curtis and Ruth discuss her out-of-state job offer and the resulting childcare dilemma in the privacy of their own home… how about if the couple wind up having the heated conversation in the middle of a couple's massage session?*

3. Revealing the truth: *Picture the scene: Harry is anxious to be meeting Esther's eco-warrior parents for the first time. He sits down on a hemp cushion for dinner at their family home and tries to make conversation by enquiring about their vegan diet. He almost chokes on his food when Esther's father*

reveals the details about their anti-consumerism 'freegan' grocery-sourcing habits.

4. Too much information: *None of us want to hear about our parent or sibling's intimate experiences… or the bladder weakness of a grandparent (especially whilst they are sitting in our new car, or on our freshly shampooed lounge suite)! Or what about the waitress who takes the time to explain why she wouldn't order the scallops?*

Below are five awkward scene-starters. Use them as prompts to inspire cringeworthy, toe-curling scenes…

- Kim and Gavin invite both sets of parents to a fancy restaurant to share the news of their engagement. However, both sets of parents had secretly hoped the relationship wouldn't last. Kim's parents despise Gavin, and Gavin's parents are less than keen on their future daughter-in-law.

- Lucy meets the friend of a friend on a bus. It's empty. They are forced to sit together. They only met briefly in passing. They cannot remember each other's name, and now they must make small talk for the rest of the journey.

- By mistake, Nick opens a letter addressed to his in-laws, Norma and Ken. He discovers the truth about a serious financial problem meaning their property is to be repossessed. As he quickly hides the letter, his wife Hannah asks her adoring parents for a loan.

- Monique has had a rough week at work. Her boss has piled on a ton of last-minute tasks and insisted she complete them before the weekend. With the jobs completed, Monique texts her friends to arrange after-work drinks – mentioning her annoying boss in the message. As she hits 'send', she realises that she has actually sent the text to her boss, instead of her friends.

Her boss is still in his office, which Monique must pass on her way out.

- Whilst they eat pizza and watch football, Dave confides in his friend Mark that he no longer loves his wife and that he has been thinking about leaving her. Judy comes home early and has been stood in the kitchen for the last five minutes, overhearing their conversation. Judy enters.

Plots Untwisted

'How dreadful the knowledge of the truth can be
when there's no help in truth.'

Oedipus Rex, Sophocles'

We all love a good plot twist, and the very best are those that pull the rug from under us and cause the audience to re-evaluate everything that's gone before, and everything we thought we knew. But chances are the writer has used foreshadowing to drop a few clues along the way, which have done a satisfactory job in setting up the twist whilst keeping it a surprise for maximum impact at just the right time. After all, a good plot twist must make sense within the context of the entire story and leave us kicking ourselves, thinking 'I should have seen that coming!' An impetuously written twist, which comes as a bolt from the blue, is more likely to disappoint the audience than excite them.

Oedipus Rex *is arguably one of the first great plot-twist plays, shocking audiences and inspiring writers for centuries. The play was based on a myth, so its original audiences might not have had quite the same surprise as modern audiences, or those unaware of the 'Oedipus Complex', but I'll avoid spoiling the twist if you're yet to read or see a production of it. Safe to say, Sophocles uses the character of the prophet Tiresias, the communication with the oracle at Delphi, and the meaning of Oedipus's name ('swollen foot' relating directly to his abandonment as a child) to foreshadow what is to come.*

Some foreshadowing is harder to spot than others, of course. M. Night Shyamalan does a great job of saving the surprise for the final few scenes of The Sixth Sense. *Other great plot twists include the 'unexpected bad guy' twist in films like* The Usual Suspects *and* Murder on the Orient Express *and conspiracy twists in* Ocean's Eleven *and* The Sting.

Of course, a twist doesn't always have to throw a spanner in the works or bring the world of the story crashing down, it can also be heartwarming. Who put two and two together about Miguel's great-great-grandfather in Coco *before the screenwriters connected the dots for us? Likewise, a twist that has real-world consequences for the protagonist can be satisfying for the audience. In* The Wizard of Oz, *we have the 'it was all a dream' twist, where Dorothy ends up learning an important lesson about home. Her waking-up at the end of the movie, together with the sepia opening, beautifully bookend her journey through Technicolor Oz.*

For this observational exercise, rewatch your favourite movie or reread a favourite play, which contained a plot twist that surprised you. Working from the very beginning, note down any subtle foreshadowing leading up to the point of the twist.

Look out for the following:

- On reflection, did the writer use deceptive dialogue?
- Did subtext help retain a veil of secrecy?
- Was subterfuge at play to divert your attention and retain the twist?

Here are some pointers for mastering foreshadowing and writing your own killer plot twist:

- Keep your clues balanced, subtle and seamless (continuity first!).
- Make your clues crucial ingredients to the story – avoid sprinkling them on top afterwards.
- A good plot twist should reveal a shocking or unexpected fact or event.
- It can't just be about surprising the audience. Your twist should also advance the plot in some way too.

- See how you can exploit a subplot either to build towards a twist or distract from the main plot whilst you set things up.

- Make sure that the story which follows the twist doesn't fall flat. Maintain the momentum you have built until the end, whenever your twist happens.

- Is there a twist you might share with the audience from the start, but hide from your characters for an even bigger pay-off? (Remember Hitchcock's ticking time-bomb.) Think of *Blood Brothers* – just like a Greek tragedy, Willy Russell reveals Mickey and Eddie's tragic fate as inevitable at the start of the play, the pay-off for the audience is the cathartic release as we witness the brothers move towards it.

- Finally, test your twist! Have a fellow writer or a supportive friend read your work. If they volunteer an encouraging *'I didn't see that coming?'* then you're probably onto a winner!

PART FOUR

IMMERSIVE WRITING

The exercises and tips in this part of the book are here to inspire your writing experience beyond the keyboard – *replacing screen time with real time!* The purpose of immersive writing is to connect with your play or screenplay through real-world experiences, digging deeper into the psyche of your characters and the worlds that they inhabit, through practical, hands-on methods. All the techniques described in these pages are tools that I regularly employ in my own writing practice. I find time away from my desk stimulating and enriching; I hope they will inspire and motivate you too.

The Writing Space

My writing room is my sanctuary. Whenever I move house, in whichever corner of the world I land, unpacking my writing space and getting it set up straight away is crucial. For me, this includes my books (scripts, poetry, resource books, biographies, etc.), my writing desks and typewriters, framed photos and posters from previous productions and behind-the-scenes memories, retired props, candles and stationery. I also reclaimed a small row of theatre seats which I sometimes like to sit back in, close my eyes and allow myself to be transported to a dark auditorium in order to visualise a piece of work on the stage.

Whatever feng shui you need, be it a desk that faces east, a Japanese beckoning cat or a string of fairy lights, assemble whatever makes you feel calm, comfortable, at your most creative – and carve out a corner that you find welcoming to work in.

Here is a rundown of the different ways that I like to work, and some of the practical things that I like to do in my writing space to stay motivated. Hopefully, there will be some new ideas that you can try yourself or adapt as you wish.

Story Wall

When I am working on a full-length play for an extended period, I like to dedicate a whole wall in my writing room to the project. This usually starts with the beat board. Using a series of different colour postcards or Post-it notes, I break down the story points into 'beats' and arrange (and rearrange) them on the wall in front of me. Sometimes I will use a ball of red yarn, replicating whatever structure I am using for my story arc on the wall itself. See the next exercise, *Post-it Plotlines* for more on this.

Once I have the bones of my story up on the wall, I will then print out photographs from the internet that relate to the people, places, props, and other things in my story, much like the crime investigation walls you see in police dramas – connecting images of people and things to the relevant areas of the story. I include maps, photos of any real contributors I might have interviewed along the way, inspiring song lyrics, and paint-colour swatches, to represent the palette I see when I visualise the world of the play. Putting the world of my story up onto the wall allows me to step back and see the bigger picture of the script and its themes as a whole. It also allows me to see the connection between characters and storylines and physically pick them up, hold them and move them around to see if a different arrangement might provide a better or more satisfying series of events.

Analogue Writing

If you, like me, write mostly on a computer, take a break from the screen and enjoy the flow of ink from a beautiful fountain pen or the precision of a nicely sharpened pencil. Something else that I have become a big fan of in recent years in the humble typewriter. I picked up an unloved Olivetti Dora off the internet a couple of years ago and haven't looked back. My collection currently includes six machines and is likely to grow. These days I try to write all of my first drafts on a typewriter, not only because I love the tapping sound of the keys and the immediacy of seeing my words planted on paper right before my eyes, but mainly because there is no delete key! This forces me to forget about editing (and overediting) and not to overthink things; instead, filling pages and pages of paper with dialogue that I can hold in my hands at the end of a writing session. There is time for prettier wordsmithing later… sometimes you just need to get the words onto the page! I can then take my typewritten draft to a coffee shop with a red pen to notate all of the things I need to address when I sit down to transcribe it later on my laptop.

Get into Character

Try bringing an item of clothing or a prop relating to your protagonist into your writing space. Whilst writing my one-act comedy-drama, *Maxine*, I placed a wig stand on my bookshelf, displaying a wig that I thought my cross-dressing character might wear. I found this helpful to look at whilst picturing certain scenes in my head. Alternatively, I might sometimes wear a cardigan, scarf or hat when I'm writing to help me to connect with a protagonist and channel their thoughts and feelings. At the time of writing, I'm working on a spec script for a television comedy-drama and have taken to sipping espresso from a martini glass in order to summon the eccentric spirit of my protagonist.

Set the Scene

You must feel relaxed when you sit down to write, leaving distractions outside of the writing space. See Part 1 for mindful meditations to help you clear your mind and re-energise your space, allowing you to be at your most positive and creative. Some people think and write better with soft music in the background, whilst others prefer complete silence. I like to write to classical piano music, smooth jazz, and occasionally a musical-theatre cast recording. Another favourite of mine is the Shipping Forecast on BBC Radio 4 (for an exercise designed around this, see *Exercise 3.4.1: Rain Later. Good, Occasionally Poor* on page 114). Perhaps the sound of passing traffic, or a thunderstorm soundscape is your preferred 'white noise'?

Lighting is also important. I love to write at night when my children are sleeping, and I can light a few candles in my space or sit by a small desk lamp. Whether you write in your own dedicated writing room or on the kitchen counter, take time to create the right ambience that will help you to feel inspired and comfortable enough to want to stay in your sanctuary.

Bring Life into Your Space

Apparently looking away from your screen to something green from time to time reduces headaches, so why not liven up your environment, and add a burst of colour with some plants? Cacti, succulents, and even faux plants are great if you don't have a lot of light, or luck, in keeping plants alive. See page 109 for an exercise on creating *A Literary Bouquet*, bringing both colour and life into your writing space.

A Change of Scenery

If I'm working at home, my drip-coffee machine is fired up in the morning and keeps me fuelled all day long. I also like to schedule at least one day in the week to write from a different location, be it a favourite coffee shop, the library, a park bench, the beach, or wherever provides a change of scenery and gets new ideas flowing. Since writing can be solitary work, it's also lovely to be around other human beings once a week. Pack up your writing tools, and a flask of coffee if you need one, and try a change of scenery. Writing on location offers different surroundings and can inspire new thoughts, especially useful if your location of choice is in any way connected to the world or one of the characters you are writing about. You will be able to capture the mood, tone, fabric and texture of the location, which could prove useful for your research and inspiring for your writing. (See *Exercise 4.3: Visiting a Soul Place* on page 169.)

Establish a Routine

Life is full of distractions, and it's all too easy to get side-tracked and not end up writing at all. I like to establish a routine, whereby I might meditate for five minutes, before either freewriting for ten minutes (see page 14), writing a six-word story (see page 149) or completing a writing prompt (see page 208). Then I sit down to work on my project. I might also take a moment to read a sonnet or a single page of a favourite script. I find this often helps me focus on the end goal (published and produced work) and reminds me why I am writing. It can be beneficial to try and carve out a regular writing routine, where the time you spend working is uninterrupted and productive. This is especially important if your writing session needs to be scheduled around housemates, a partner or children and animals.

Post-it Plotlines

Stage and screen are visual mediums, and sometimes it helps to step back and view plotlines and subplotlines in full, at a macro level, whilst planning, writing and rewriting. First, let's just recap on the difference and importance of each:

- *Plot is your main story arc – what happens from beginning to end. Plot provides the main action, characters, motivations and conflicts. It also informs the audience of the central themes, symbols and motifs. In a nutshell, stories revolve around the main plot.*

- *Subplot is a secondary plot or series of side stories which often run parallel to the unfolding action in the main plot. Subplots can add complications, obstacles or additional conflict for a protagonist (or antagonist) and provide reinforcement to the main plot. Subplots can also be used to underline themes, fill holes and impart information about the principal characters and the main plot that may not otherwise be revealed. See Exercise 3.5.5: Baked to Plotfection on page 143.*

Mounting your plotlines on a wall will allow you to stand back and view your story as a whole; to touch it and move it around easily. David Mamet is said to use cork boards with sheets of butcher paper or index cards in order to work out his plot progressions.

Find a roll of paper (cheap wallpaper, decorating backing paper, or florists' wrapping paper are great for this), and cut it to the full length of an empty wall in your writing space and use mounting putty to fix it to the wall temporarily at a height you can easily reach. If I'm working on a screenplay, I find it helpful at this stage to draw Syd Field's screenplay paradigm (shown over the page) in a marker pen across the full length of the paper, giving a guiding structure in the background.

Similarly, you might also try using Freytag's Pyramid (see page 130).

Next, you will need two different colour Post-it note pads. On one colour pad, write down every plot point in your script and place the notes roughly along the wall in the order that they occur. On the second colour pad, write down every subplot point and add these notes to the wall too. Now it's time to get hands-on! I love this process because it makes your story into something tangible.

On the following page you can see an example of plotline Post-it notes laid out on Syd Field's screenplay paradigm.

Seeing your plotlines and subplotlines laid out before you, stand back and notice the spacing of the two colours. Does anything jump out to you? Is one section of the wall looking a little overcrowded whilst the other is looking a little lonely? Would it make more sense to have certain events happen over here rather than over there? Sooner rather than later? Is less more?

Get physical with your story. Step into it and move the Post-it notes, adding new ones to plug holes and really shake things up. Question everything. Which plotlines or subplotlines drive your script forward? Do any of them hold it back in parts or work counter to the overall dramatic structure? Is the conflict in your plot balanced with sufficient reversal to maintain an emotional connection with the audience? Are any parts of your plot too 'busy' or overly complicated? Returning to view your wall after some time away is useful too. Does a good night's sleep and fresh eyes change anything?

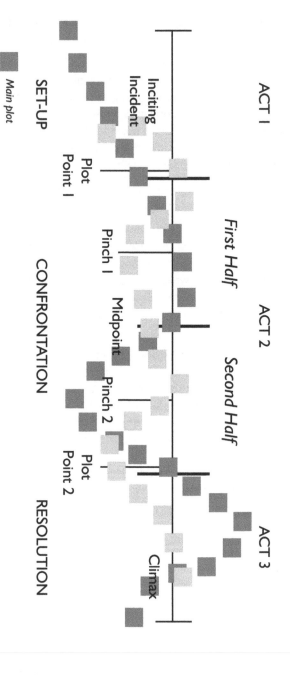

ACT I

ACT 2

ACT 3

SET-UP

CONFRONTATION

RESOLUTION

First Half

Second Half

Inciting Incident

Plot Point 1

Pinch 1

Midpoint

Pinch 2

Plot Point 2

Climax

Main plot

Subplot

Visiting a Soul Place

I first became interested in immersive writing when researching my first verbatim play, The Countess, *in 2014 – a project that required me to leave my desk and go out into the field and make contact with the living people in the story and to visit the actual locations where the scenes played out. I found the experience so profound and stimulating for my writing practice that I now incorporate these techniques into all of my work, regardless of the style or genre of the piece. This is no longer limited to my research period, but something I employ throughout the writing process where possible.*

The purpose of this is to add texture to your writing by connecting with the physical world of your script – an immersive experience allowing you to absorb an authentic feel of a place. Many times, such experiences can lead to informative meetings, new information and rich new material.

The important thing to remember when deciding on your location, or 'soul place', is that you must be able to connect with the heart of your story and use it as an entry point to the world you are creating or capturing.

Step 1: Decide on Your Soul Place

You will be undertaking a period of observational research, in a location relating to the world of your play, screenplay or story. For example, my play *The Countess* centres around a café in Roundwood Park in Harlesden, North London. Since this was the common ground between my characters and was the place that brought everyone together, the café itself offered a microcosm or epicentre within which to tell the story, and a starting point to begin my research.

It is not always possible to visit the exact location where your story takes place, or where you might imagine it to take place, especially if it is a faraway location, or if the world is fictional. In this case, I would encourage you to find somewhere that closely resembles the world within your story or a place that will at least allow you to imagine your world. For example, if your story is set during World War One, perhaps you can undertake your observational research at a war museum, a park memorial, or at a wartime festival or battle enactment. If your story takes place at sea, you might visit a beach or harbour. If you are writing a modern-day, naturalistic piece, then maybe you will choose to spend time at a launderette, on a bus, or in a hospital waiting room. In order to absorb a sense of the legal proceedings within *The Countess*, I also spent time watching court cases play out in Harrow Crown Court.

Here are some pointers to check that your time spent in this location will be beneficial and productive:

- Is your choice of location rich in visual and aural potential?

- Are there strong atmospheric qualities?

- Does the location suggest story potential and narrative possibilities?

Step 2: Immerse and Collect

If possible, plan to stagger your visits to the location over a period of time, and at different times of day and night (if appropriate). You will find the following tools useful to take with you:

- Physical writing materials.

- Pencils and a sketch-pad.

- Camera.

- Dictaphone or mobile phone you can record audio on.

Find a comfortable place to sit and allow your mind to empty, making space for a deep connection with the location around you. Allow yourself to become a sponge, absorbing every drop of activity within this environment. Through notes, recordings, photographs and sketches, begin to collect material that may seem mundane or prosaic, but which will help you to add layers of texture to your writing.

For me, visiting Roundwood Lodge Café meant sitting at a quiet table and observing the voices of customers ordering at the counter, the sound of the cash register, noises from the kitchen, staff calling out order numbers on the PA system, and music and chat from a local radio station playing softly in the background. I was imagining the conversations that would have played out inside the four walls of the café. I left my Dictaphone recording, and whilst I wasn't looking for 'dialogue' per se, I was picking up the style and patterns of speech, the variety of accents, and the sounds and ambience of the café. I also noted the sun spilling through the windows in the morning, highlighting different parts of the space, projecting patterns of the trees outside onto the vinyl table covering and reflecting through the glass cruet set. I noted the smell of bacon cooking, coffee brewing and sweet cakes on the countertop. All the while, I was clutching a mug of coffee, thinking about the characters in my story who might have used that same mug, those who may have even washed it, dried it or filled it with tea or coffee. All of this provided me with a real 'sense of place' that I might have been unable to understand had I not visited the venue in person.

Should you decide to break from being a fly on the wall, you may find it insightful to speak with people in the space. Listening to their stories and finding out about their personal connections to the place may inspire or inform the backstories of your characters and their environments.

Step 3: Application

Once you have completed a period of research, it's time to think about distilling and collating this material, going through a selection process, and making creative editorial judgements about how your observations can be used to enhance your work. After a period of observational research, I always feel an immense rush of inspiration and try to hurry home, scribbling away into my notebook as ideas pour from my mind and onto the page. It's an exhilarating feeling. Here are some questions to think about as you continue this process:

- Did the location evoke a sense of interior landscape – what colours, styles, decor and furnishings were specific to the place? You can use this knowledge to invite the reader into the world of your story by adding this information to your play's stage directions, or to the action of a screenplay.

- How might the sounds you observed at the location inform the individual verbal personalities, speech patterns and quirks of your characters? Any atmospheric sounds which you might include in your work will all help transport the reader.

- What was the mood and tone of the location? Does this speak to a sense of ease or unrest in the scenes you are writing? Is this something that you might use to crank up dramatic tension on the page?

- Perhaps the lighting, or lack of, will play an essential part in telling your story, affecting how a scene unfolds and the actions of your characters.

With my second verbatim play, *In the Tall Grass*, which charts the ever-increasing murder rate of transgender women of colour across the United States, I was able to take my time in the field to a whole new level. The play focuses on the murder of Dallas woman Shade Schuler, the national epidemic serving as a backdrop. I directed the world premiere of the play in Dallas, Texas, in 2017 and during rehearsals, I was able to take the cast to visit notable locations and introduce them to the real-life people whom they were portraying on stage. On two occasions, I even directed scenes from the play at sites where the actual events of the story took place. This was a uniquely powerful and grounding experience for the cast, who were able to bring this to their performances, adding layers of authenticity and depth to the harrowing story.

Whilst we are not focused on trying to write scenes during our observational research period, you may enjoy, as I do, making further visits to a location once you have digested your initial research to spend time writing your script in situ.

IMMERSIVE WRITING

Method Writing

'The further you get away from yourself, the more challenging it is. Not to be in your comfort zone is great fun.'

Benedict Cumberbatch

Russian actor and theatre director, Konstantin Stanislavsky (1863–1938) set out a series of techniques, still used by actors today, to portray emotions on stage by putting themselves in the place of their characters. We often hear about actors going to great lengths to find their characters, by honing specialist skills, learning survival tactics and embarking on extreme diets. Adrien Brody famously lost thirty pounds and learned to play the piano (practising for four hours a day!) to play Holocaust survivor Władysław Szpilman in The Pianist. *Robert De Niro reportedly got his taxi driver's licence and would pick up passengers in New York City during his breaks from filming* Taxi Driver. *For her role in* Jungle Fever, *Halle Berry claimed to have visited a crack den and not washed for two weeks.*

Writing is, by nature, an immersive experience, so I believe there is much that writers can also take away from Stanislavsky's methods in the 'art of experiencing' and apply them to our process.

Method Writer (*noun*)
'A writer or author who uses a technique of writing in which he/she identifies emotionally with a character in the story and assumes that character's persona in the telling. This writing style allows insights into a character's motives, reactions and thoughts that usually can only be inferred from other styles. Authors using this technique may describe the sensation of writing as if they were spiritually channelling the character.'
(*Urban Dictionary*)

Whilst most writers only mentally immerse themselves in the roles they create, some like to take things a step further. Thomas W. Hodgkinson, the founder of the Method Writers Project, is one such writer. Here is an excerpt of an interview he gave to BBC Radio 4 in 2016:

'I wrote the bulk of my new novel, *Memoirs of a Stalker*, whilst lying flat on my back in one of the cupboards in my home. There wasn't even room for a laptop, so I had to write it on my mobile phone… I was trying to get into the mindset of my main character, who breaks into his ex-girlfriend's house and lives there for months without her knowing. He spends a lot of time lurking in shadows, behind doors, and crouched in cupboards.'

If you don't fancy hiding in a cupboard for weeks on end, here are a few 'level one' suggestions, for how you might dip your toe in the water and see if method-writing techniques aid your process.

Shopping List

The late, great Victoria Wood once joked that if she wasn't in the mood for shopping, she would just follow someone else around the supermarket and buy whatever they were buying. As part of your character-profiling/creation process, try writing a shopping list, including whatever you think your character would buy. Then, as an immersive experience, channel your character as you walk the aisles of your local supermarket and complete their grocery shop. You may choose to return the items to the shelves and finish the exercise there, or, alternatively, check-out and eat dinner in role as your character. Use this exercise to explore and connect with your character on a physical level to discover facets of their character that you may not have considered before.

A Comfy Pair of Slippers

Try choosing your own outfit for the day through the eyes of your character. Does wearing a beret help you to form a deeper connection when writing a touching scene involving a soldier returning home from war? Perhaps a favourite pair of slippers or the borrowed cardigan of an elderly relative will provide you with warmth and sentimentality; or maybe the scent of a baby blanket can evoke memories or a sense of place that you will be able to channel into your writing.

More Tea, Vicar?

Does your character have a favourite drink? If you are writing a Christmas-themed play or screenplay, then perhaps sipping a peppermint hot chocolate with marshmallows will help you to get into the festivities and summon a Yuletide spirit. Or maybe your character is always seen nursing a cup of tea, or something stronger perhaps? Whether you drink it, or simply set a glass of something significant down on your desk as inspiration, try bringing tangible tastes, smells and props from your character's life into your own.

Caffè Macchiato for Mercutio?

Next time your friendly barista asks for a name to scribble on your coffee cup, pluck up the confidence to offer up your character's name instead. You might even forsake your usual drink and consider what they might order.

Cookson or King?

Supposing you were to browse the shelves at your local library in role as your character, what might be their book of choice? Whether *The Rag Nymph* or *The Shining*, borrow a book you think they might read and disappear between the pages, reading the words and interpreting them as your character would themselves. After all, we are all informed by the places we visit, the people we meet and the sights, sounds and information we absorb every day. Try the same principle when deciding what film to watch next, or which song or radio station to listen to.

'No writer just sits down at a desk without any preparation. What we're saying is be creative about your preparation, even at the cost of seeming a little bit ridiculous… But many of the great method actors have been laughed at, and they didn't turn out too bad in the end.'

Thomas W. Hodgkinson

For more information on Thomas W. Hodgkinson's work, visit his website: www.thomaswhodgkinson.com

Get Social

'Fantasy is hardly an escape from reality. It's a way of understanding it.'

Lloyd Alexander

These exercises are designed to bring offline method-writing principles, as in the previous exercise, into the online world.

Once you have created a clear character profile (see *Exercise 3.1.1: Getting to Know You* on page 36), try the following ideas as a way to extend your understanding of your character's thoughts, feelings, wants and desires – and curate them as a digital footprint or collage of your character.

Social Media

A Twitter profile, created in the name of your character, is an easy way to post in role, allowing you to capture sudden moments of inspiration, such as a magical line of dialogue, thought or feeling and push it out into the world. So long as your character is inoffensive, publishing short dialogue ideas, quotes, poems or idioms in character is a useful way to personify your characters. I have a Twitter account for one of my favourite characters and have allowed their spirit to live on beyond the play from which they originated, by posting little ditties under this pseudonym every so often. Likewise, a dedicated Instagram profile will allow you to post images through the eyes of a character.

Scrapbook

Pinterest is a handy tool for collating images, quotes and sources of inspiration for your play. I like to create different boards for each of my characters, as well as a board for the settings and themes of my projects, pinning photographs and ideas which I might later print out and include on the story wall in my writing room (see page 161). Things to pin to a character's Pinterest board might include postcards from family vacations, a childhood pet, a soft toy, a wedding photo, baby photos, items of clothing, cars, personal possessions, a work uniform. Likewise, for a location, I might create a board where I can pin photographs which help to evoke a strong sense of place, including landscapes, sky colour, weather conditions, culture, local cuisine, regional style/art/design, local people, flags, architecture, plants and so on.

Dating Profile

If your character were looking for love, how would they describe themselves on a dating site? (My suggestion is to try this exercise offline, on paper!) As you pen the perfect profile, here are some things to think about:

- What are they passionate about?

- What do they care most about in the world?

- What fills them with excitement?

- How do they fill their spare time and what does a typical day off work look like?

- Do they have a charitable or philanthropic side?

- What do they love most about themselves and what would they change?

- What are their weaknesses and/or vulnerabilities?

- What are they looking for in a relationship and what would their perfect partner's attributes include?

- How would their nearest and dearest describe them?

- When did they last date?

- How quickly or slowly do they like to take things?

Dear Diary

Something else I like to do whilst working on a full-length or larger piece of work is to keep a daily journal in the voice of my protagonist. By checking in with your characters for five minutes at the end of each writing session, you can process the developments they have made in the scene or scenes you have been working on, whether in their character arc, story arc or both. I use a pocket-sized notebook for this, preferring to close my laptop and write by hand at the end of the day, but you might prefer to keep a digital diary in a document. You could also write a short daily blog, publishing your protagonist's thoughts to share online with your writing network.

PART FIVE

THE TEN-MINUTE PLAY

Ten-minute plays are great fun to read, to write, and to watch. As an audience member, a showcase of short vignettes can be very entertaining – *plus, if you don't enjoy one… it will be over very quickly!* As a writer, they present an opportunity to sit down and write a complete play (or at least a rough and ready first draft) in one sitting; since the goal is roughly ten pages of dialogue. They can be useful to have in your portfolio of work to use as a calling card, or to enter into playwriting festivals and competitions, helping you to get your work on stage relatively easily and start to build a writing resumé.

Writing a good ten-minute play, however, is a challenge. How can you present a complete story, with a satisfying story arc that hits all of the right notes, whilst sticking to the strict page count? For me, the secret is in the plot! Not every story can, or should, be told in ten minutes and so your plot needs careful consideration. But if you finish your ten-minute play and feel that it has potential to be something bigger, why not flesh it out further and explore the idea of developing it into a one-act or even full-length piece? Sometimes starting small can be a great way to try out a bigger idea.

5.1 The Perfect Ten

We are going to write a ten-minute play, focusing primarily on plot for the purpose of this exercise. Once your script holds up to the unique demands of the ten-minute format, you can spend time fleshing out your characters and finessing their dialogue.

Below is a blueprint for a basic ten-page story structure, designed to ensure that each page serves a purpose and advances the plot. Since real estate on your page is at a premium, my top tip is to keep the plot focused, ensuring every detail on the page is relevant to the action of the story – there is no time for anything extraneous.

Page 1: Hit the ground running

You don't have time or space to set up characters or share their backstories, so forget about exposition and jump straight into the story. Introduce the 'trigger' that sets the story in motion from the off, and even better, join the story during the fallout from something that's already happened (see *Exercise 3.2.4: I'll Join You for Dessert* on page 79). Bonus points if you can open with an image or motif that might be seen again at the end for a sense of unity or resolve.

Page 2–3: The challenge is set

As a result of the trigger, the protagonist is forced to 'fix' or 'find' something, and so the journey at the heart of the play is established, and the audience is engaged to come along for the ride. A door is opened that cannot be closed and there is no turning back (see *Exercise 3.5.3: Did You Lock the Door?* on page 138).

Page 3–5: Speedbump

There is a problem, a snag or a hurdle in the way, meaning that getting from A to B is not going to be as simple as we first thought. Enter the antagonist or antagonistic force. Your protagonist will probably spend these few pages dealing with this conflict or obstacle.

Page 6–7: Curveball

With your protagonist on the cusp of restoring order to their world, they are thrown another curveball and face a difficult decision. Don't let them off easily!

Page 8–9: Pinnacle

The climax is reached, but not without cost or consequence, and the ultimate transformation, change or lesson for your protagonist and/or their world is realised.

Page 10: Denouement

Battles are won or lost, either way, matters are explained or resolved. Did you get your bonus point for closing with the opening image? If there was an unopened bottle of Champagne with two glasses on stage at the start of the play, somehow let's return to this image at the end. Is the bottle empty? Has it been smashed? Have one of the glasses gone? You decide!

PART SIX

SUBMISSION SURGERY

Congratulations! You've done it! Characters, their stories and their world have been created in your vision. You have committed them to text, and so they exist. Take a moment to recognise this milestone. Whether your script is at first, second or third-draft stage, go ahead and print it out. Make it tangible. Hold it. Hug it.

So, you've written your script. Now what?

The road to production is different for every script, and every writer. What that end goal looks like, and how we get there depends on how we see our work, what we want for it, and the steps we take to get it there. If you are a relatively new playwright, you will no doubt be hungry to get your work on stage. If so, take advantage of the vast number of new-writing festivals and competitions. Whilst each of them differ greatly in terms of production, as well as the scope for professional development and investment in you and your work, what they will almost certainly provide is a chance to work alongside a producer, director and actors in getting your work on stage and in front of an audience. Submitting to festivals is also a great way to give yourself delivery deadlines, which are a real motivator, as well as credits which you can use to start to build your playwriting resumé.

Likewise, screenwriting festivals and contests offer great opportunities. Best case, you might get your script in front of an equally passionate producer or director who is keen to talk further and who could help you to realise your script as a finished short film, giving you a calling card for use in communications for other opportunities. Worst case, you might get some useful 'script coverage' (feedback) which you can use to advance the next draft. If you are interested in networking with filmmakers, explore websites like Raindance, Mandy and Shooting People. Another route to realising your short film screenplay, or even a strong stand-alone scene from a full-length screenplay, is to self-produce a micro-budget film through collaboration with others.

George Lucas is believed to have said a movie is never finished, only abandoned. A quote that is attributed to the French poet Paul Valéry before him, with regards to poetry, and Leonardo da Vinci before him, when speaking about art. Whenever it was first said, and by whom, the sentiment is painfully just. As a painter might stand back and look at their work, never entirely satisfied and keen to tweak… and tweak some more, writers can no doubt see potential edits each and every time we reread our scripts. However, at some point, if we want our work to move forward we must put it before readers who are in a position to help us achieve our goals for the piece, be they producers, directors or otherwise. Hitting 'send' on an email, or 'submit' on a submission web form can be angst-ridden for a writer. The script that you have pained over, lived, and breathed every waking (and sleeping!) moment since you first sat down to write it, is about to be pushed out into the big wide world and it must stand on its own feet for the first time.

The exercises in this part are all geared towards helping you make sure your script is the best it can be before it leaves your computer. Regardless of where, or to whom you are sending your work, use the tips in this part as a litmus test for your script, before submission.

Trimming the Fat

> 'Substitute 'damn' every time you're inclined to write 'very';
> your editor will delete it, and the writing will be just as it
> should be.'
>
> *Mark Twain*

Do some scenes feel a little sluggish in areas? Could they do with a bit of tightening? Never fear, this next exercise will help you take a microscope to your dialogue… followed by a very sharp scalpel! Here, pace is the name of the game. If a line of dialogue doesn't move the story along, enhance the audience's understanding of a scene or tell us something we need to know… then maybe your scene can live without it.

In this exercise on 'letting go', I describe how to apply this principle to a brand new scene as a writing exercise, but you can also apply it to a working draft.

Cut out a photograph from a newspaper or magazine featuring two people in the foreground. Any scenario is fine – e.g. an elderly couple on the beach, a parent and child baking, two people on a bus, two soldiers in combat… anything you like. Take a moment to study the photograph. Let's call these two characters 'A' and 'B'.

Next, take a ruled notebook or sheet of writing paper and write A and B (instead of character names) in your page margins a total of eighteen times – so that characters A and B each get nine lines of dialogue. Now write a quick exchange of dialogue between A and B. By restricting the conversation to one line per character in a simple back and forth exchange, you will remove the temptation to overthink things. Just look at the photo and write whatever you hear! No one else is going to read this scene – your characters can chat about the best way to fry fish, or how to diffuse a bomb, it really doesn't matter.

Done? Okay. Time to get brutal. Here's the knife. You are only allowed to keep a total of ten lines of dialogue! You cannot reorder or edit any of the lines. Read through your scene and simply strike through eight lines, saving only the ten that you feel are absolutely essential to telling the story as efficiently as possible. It doesn't matter if character B ends up speaking two of their lines back-to-back. No editing allowed!

Now read your new scene. What are your thoughts? Did the essence of the scene survive? Does it hold up despite the liberal cuts? If so, maybe the lines you just cut were helpful during the writing process and have now served their purpose. Chances are that by removing superfluous dialogue, a cleaner, leaner scene remains.

As an additional exercise, print or write out a scene from a well-known play or screenplay, or transcribe a thirty-second scene from a movie or television show. Can you cut five or six lines and create a tighter exchange?

Dialogue Don'ts

Writing great dialogue can be hard work. You might have a fantastic plot and perfectly crafted characters, but if your reader's toes are curling at cringeworthy clichés and inane exchanges, they may not make it past the first few pages of your script. So, before you hit the send button… scan your script in search of the following 'dialogue dont's':

- Avoid 'info-dumping' large amounts of exposition in dialogue; it reads as lazy. For help with exposition, see *Exercise 3.5.1: Invisible Exposition* on page 132.

- If an essential piece of information is imparted, and the success of your story depends on the audience picking it up, you need to make sure it lands. As a rule of thumb, use the 'rule of three', repeating this information three times during your script, in different ways, to make it stick. This can be physically, visually, verbally or even in subtext. Don't lay it on thick… just make sure it's in there. You never want to have to explain afterwards, something that was fundamental to the audience's enjoyment and understanding of the story.

- *'Hello, Danny.' 'Hi, Sue!' 'Have you eaten, Danny? Fancy some chips?' 'No, thanks, Sue, I've just had a big lunch'.* Yes, you got it… avoid overusing character names. In real life, we rarely use someone's name when talking to them directly, reserving names for those not present or involved in the conversation. Overuse of names can sound silly and be the mark of an inexperienced writer. The exception, perhaps, is if addressing people by name is part of your character's nature, or if it's a regional practice or a stylistic choice. Once you have established a character's name early on, use it economically going forward.

- Be wary of small talk. *'I like your scarf'* may fill an awkward silence, but it doesn't advance the plot. Likewise, too much talk about the past doesn't push the story forwards. Better to focus on what's next and how we're going to get there.

- Interruption is key... it's the difference between a monologue and dialogue. Just as people interject, talk over one another and comment whilst someone else is talking, avoid characters making verbose speeches without interruption.

- I won't 'beat around the bush' with this one – avoid using trite phrases and clichés... like the plague!! If your characters live 'happily ever after', chances are your script won't. So keep dialogue original and inspired.

- Be consistent with dialogue, keeping it character-specific. As a test, cover up the character names in your script and make sure that you can still tell who's talking.

- This list would not be complete without a reminder of the 'show, don't tell' rule. Instead of Bev shouting, *'Cook your own dinner, Tony, I'm done',* better have her slam the casserole dish down on the counter, take off her apron and pour a large glass of wine.

Scenes on Trial

Once you have a complete draft of your script, look at each of your scenes individually, interrogate them, and ask some fundamental questions in order to find out what sticks... and what stinks!

Every scene should achieve at least one of the following:

- *Establish a mood or tone.*
- *Advance or complicate the plot.*
- *Connect plot points.*
- *Establish relationships between characters.*
- *Reveal new information.*
- *Reveal a theme or motif.*
- *Entertain.*
- *Create pathos.*

They say writing is rewriting, and if you're like me, the thrill of completing your first draft can very quickly disappear when you sit down to work on your second. Fear not... follow this twenty-point checklist to help you get a handle on the structure and content of your scenes.

1. Is the *setting* clear? Does the reader/audience know where they are, and why?

2. How are the *themes* of your script represented in the scene?

3. Are the *connections* of the characters in the scene clear?

4. What is the *objective of the scene* in the overall story arc? Does the scene help to reveal something new about the characters or plot?

5. What are the *objectives of the characters* in the scene, and how do they serve their *super-objectives*?

6. Do all of the characters have *distinct voices* in the scene?

7. What about the *voice of the script* as a whole? Does the dialogue clearly convey the mood, tone and style of voice you had in mind at the start of the writing process?

8. What/where is the *subtext* of the scene? In the main story beat and/or dialogue?

9. Where is the *power* in the scene – which characters are passive and which are active?

10. Where is the *conflict/complication* in the scene? What is creating the *drama*?

11. Are the *stakes* of the scene objective and the *consequences* for the protagonist still clear? Double-check they haven't become diluted, muddied or lost along the way. Maybe even take the chance to raise them?

12. Are the *plots and subplots* of the scene playing in harmony, enhancing and complementing one another?

13. Does the scene have solid *foundations* – a beginning, middle and end?

14. How does the scene *transition* into the next? Is it smooth, or does it jar? Try to avoid leaving a scene abruptly and just crashing into the next.

15. Is the *chronology* of the scene present and correct? Does the reader/audience know, or need to know, how much time has passed?

16. What about *continuity*? If your plot is complex or has detail that needs to be watertight, then I recommend a separate continuity read to check for leaks, and to plug any holes before you submit your script. A second pair of eyes is useful here too – if you have an eagle-eyed friend

who always knows who the killer is and likes to ruin a good movie, why not ask them to have a read?

17. Is the scene *satisfying*? Does it *hold* the audience? Is there a natural *hook* to the next scene?

18. What is *special* about this scene? Does it offer *something extra*? An element of surprise, a twist, or an interesting motif?

19. Does the scene strike an *emotional* chord? A good scene should make the reader/audience feel something. *Anything!* Do we empathise, feel pride, experience sorrow, squirm in our seat, become awkward or laugh?

20. Identify a single overarching emotion for each scene in your script and list them in order. Look at the list and define the *emotional journey* on which you are sending the reader/audience. This may prompt you to reconsider the order of scenes.

The Logline Test

6.4

Have you ever been in a situation where you start describing your current work in progress to someone, and halfway through you realise that there is a gaping hole in your plot, or that it just doesn't sound as amazing when you say it out loud?

A logline is a brief (usually one-sentence) summary of your project which emphasises what makes your story unique, thus stimulating interest. Loglines are used when talking to industry professionals in networking environments and in correspondence.

Loglines are most commonly used in screenwriting as opposed to playwriting, but regardless of the medium, the ability to boil your plot down into a short, snappy and exciting sentence is an incredibly useful skill.

Write a gripping logline for your current work in progress which is immediately unique and engaging. As a rule of thumb, they should be a maximum of fifty words – though less is definitely more – and you should aim to include these four key elements:

- *Who* is the protagonist at the centre of the story?
  - A shamed lawyer, a psychic poodle, a child genius, etc.
- *What* is their goal/want/desire?
  - To clear their name, to find a missing person, to find a cure for an illness, etc.
- *Why* can't they get it? Who or what is standing in their way?
  - A crazy ex-lover, the end of the world, etc.
- *Where* does the story take place?
  - Some scripts operate in a world with specific rules and require a brief set-up to explain them, e.g. 'In a world

where all children are banished to live underground by an evil dictator…' Or sometimes the protagonist's backstory is crucial to the plot and needs to be included: 'suffering a nervous breakdown…' or 'after being wrongly accused…', etc.

Where possible, adding a ticking time-bomb to your logline is a great way to add urgency to your story and raise the stakes even more. For example: To win back his family and save Christmas, a shamed lawyer must clear the names of seven in-store Santas accused of stealing merchandise before Christmas Eve.

You shouldn't reveal the ending in a logline – save this for the script! The story must be good enough to hold up by itself. Remember, the purpose of the logline is not to tell the story, it is to *sell* the story. Your primary focus is to create a desire to read the script.

Writing a logline before you start writing your first draft is a great way to check that your story idea stands up. Chances are if you struggle to write a logline, then writing the script will feel like an uphill struggle.

I hope this will help you to write a sharp and intriguing 'elevator pitch', so the next time you are asked, *'So, what are you working on at the moment?'*, you will be ready to sell your story. You may only have someone's ear for thirty seconds… so make it count!

The Pizza Read

Books are written to be read. Scripts are written to be performed!

Okay… so you have done the hard yards. You now have a script that is in good shape, and you are starting to think about the next steps on the road to production. If I can offer one piece of advice above all others in this book, it is the importance of hearing your words off the page. Very often, as the writer of the work, you will have read and reread your script so many times that you start to miss or overlook things. Published authors don't go to print without the keen eye of their editor giving their book a full MOT. Likewise, your script shouldn't progress on its journey to stage or screen without a thorough bill of health.

Errors, timing issues, inconsistencies, duff lines, gags that don't land, and lost moments can often go unnoticed by merely reading the script yourself. So, before you hit the send or submit button, why not arrange a reading with members of your valued writing network or a willing cast of actors?

Okay, sure… but what's pizza got to do with it?

Pizza reads are one of my favourite things, a significant milestone to look forward to when working towards a finished draft. They provide an excellent opportunity to get my writer and actor friends together and to share my work with them. You should find your friends will be only too happy to get together for a script reading and help you to progress your craft. By positioning your reading as a 'pizza read', you are offering something in return for everyone's time, whilst keeping things friendly and informal. It doesn't cost a lot to have a couple of large pizzas in the middle of the table, turning an unpaid schlep on the subway on a soggy Sunday evening into a creative get-together. Pizza and the chance to read an exciting new script… who could refuse?

Of course, hearing your work aloud in close quarters can also be incredibly nerve-wracking, so having a large slice of Margherita to hide behind certainly helps. I have always found the outcome incredibly valuable and I encourage you to make pizza reads a regular event in your writing process.

Below are my top fifteen tips for a successful pizza read:

1. If finances are tight, you can always host your reading at home. However, if you can budget for it, I recommend booking a small rehearsal room or studio. Alternatively, check with your local library – they often have private study rooms which can be booked for free... just make sure it's okay to bring food! Wherever you go, make sure the space has a table large enough for everyone to sit around comfortably.

2. Avoid locations where noise will spill over from adjoining rooms.

3. Get access to the room thirty minutes ahead of your start time so that you have time to set up. Place chairs in a circle with a table in the middle to put your pizzas on.

4. Make sure you remember where the room is if you are visiting the venue for the first time and find out where the toilets are. Also, be sure to make a note of the keycode if there is one. I offer this word of caution from personal experience, having once been stranded on the street for thirty minutes with eight actors and five large pizzas after a door locked behind me when I went outside to let someone in. Very embarrassing. Not ideal. Don't get locked out!

5. Nobody is expecting a sit-down dinner, but you should provide bottled water for each reader and some light nibbles. It doesn't need to be pizza, of course – just be a good host and let your team know that you appreciate them.

6. Whilst the first reading of any sort is always cold, a freezing-cold read can just be flat and unhelpful. I always try to email the script out to my readers a week ahead of the date. You should stress that there is no need to learn anything, but by sending it ahead of time, you are at least giving everyone the chance to have familiarised themselves in advance with the story and the character that you would like them to read.

7. I used to make sure I always printed copies of the script for everyone, just to avoid the hassle and expense on their part. However, if you send the script ahead of time, some people will choose to print a copy at home. I now say in my email that I will bring copies for anyone who needs one and ask them to let me know if they would prefer to print their own. This way, you are not left with eight unused scripts and sustainability guilt.

8. Make an audio recording of the reading for reference when working on your next draft. I always let the readers know I am doing this, in case anyone has an issue. Nobody ever has. You can note this in your invitation email, or simply remind the group before you hit record on your phone or Dictaphone.

9. Think about casting. If you are fortunate to know a lot of actors, consider the kind of actors you imagine in the roles, and cast appropriately from your talent pool. If you are not able to cast the roles from those you know, reach out to your network and ask if anyone knows someone who fits the bill. Far better to cast an older actor for an older role than have a fresh-faced graduate read the part. Working this way also provides an opportunity to see and hear certain actors in the roles whom you might like to take forward with the project. A number of the actors who have appeared in my work have been involved with projects from the pizza read onwards. This also gives them a real investment in the piece and the origination of

the character. For smaller roles, consider casting fellow writers. Having their eyes on the script and subsequent feedback from the reading will be invaluable!

10. Don't read one of the characters yourself! Reading is multitasking, and it doesn't allow you to focus solely on listening, which is what you are there to do. Listen out for rhythm, pace and nuance – all the things you can't pick up on when reading yourself at home.

11. Likewise, cast an additional person who can read in the stage directions and actions. You shouldn't do this yourself either. This additional person will also provide a useful understudy, should someone cancel.

12. As you are listening to the reading, try to hear the words from an audience's perspective. Does it sound how you imagined? Are plot points and subplots clear? Is the dialogue smooth, convincing and compelling? Are the scene transitions working as they need to? Are fundamental character traits coming across?

13. Avoid the awkward bit at the end. Before you start reading, set out your expectations with regards to feedback to avoid everyone feeling obliged to say favourable things and praise your work at the end. What I find works best is to ask everyone at the beginning to make any notes on their script as they are reading. State that instead of taking feedback at the end, you will send everyone a link to complete an online questionnaire which you have prepared. You can create a free questionnaire on Google Forms, which people can then complete anonymously if they choose. By doing this, you save everyone from an uncomfortable exchange, and ensure that the feedback you receive is honest and considered. You also free your reader up to leave on time, as reading a full-length script with a break in the middle can be quite enough for one evening.

14. Always send a friendly follow-up email to your readers, thanking them for their time and talents, and promising to keep them in the loop with development news. It is nice to hear what is happening with a piece to which you gave your time. This is also a good opportunity to share the link to your online questionnaire.

15. *Make sure you have some vegetarian pizzas!*

PART SEVEN

QUICK-FIRE 101

Writing a short scene off the top of your head can set you up for a productive writing session, or a great way to meet a daily writing challenge when you don't feel like sitting down to a more significant piece of writing.

This part of the book comprises 101 quick-fire writing prompts for super-speedy two-minute scenes. You can use them to provide a break in the middle of a big project, or as a distraction from writer's block. Simply pick one, free your mind, and let the words flow!

There is no time to overthink anything here – there are no rules and nothing is wrong. This writing is for your eyes only.

101 Writing Prompts

001. ¡Arte Español!

Julie, an American who has been resident in Madrid for many years, gives a tour of the national Prado art museum to visiting friends, none of whom are in the slightest bit interested (but do they admit it?). *Write the scene!*

002. The Apology

Best friends Dirk and Rita have not spoken for five weeks. He blames her for not telling him straight away about his cheating boyfriend, Ross. She is annoyed he has forgiven Ross, but not her. Dirk visits Rita to apologise but somehow manages to make things worse. *Write the scene!*

003. Do I Know You?

Waking up in hospital after a severe head injury, Moira is visited by the driver of the car that left her in a coma for two months. She doesn't remember anything. Does the driver still apologise for the accident? *Write the scene!*

004. Sonia Sings

The morning after Sonia participated in a stage hypnotist act in Las Vegas, she sits down with her friend Babs for breakfast in a hotel dining room. Babs realises something is not quite right when Sonia sings her order to the waiter. *Write the scene!*

005. A Vintage Tale

Pick up a bottle of wine. Write a short story set in the country of origin, in the year of vintage, using words from the label description to dictate the mood and tone of the story. *Write the story!*

006. Charity Begins at Home

Over dinner with her adult children, Connie announces that she has written a will and will be leaving her entire estate to a Sri Lankan street-dog charity. *Write the scene!*

007. Penny the Poet

At her poetry group meeting, Penny stands to share a new verse with the group. It includes the words: water, ripple, stone, babbling, delicate, floral and sunshine… yet manages to offend everyone. What did she write?! *Write the poem (and the scene)!*

008. Outfoxed

A pack of foxhounds have decided that their canine connection to foxes is stronger than their relationship with humans. As two hunters in their scarlet riding jackets canter through the countryside, the sound of their bugle brings an unexpected result. *Write the scene!*

009. Stuck

Nadia irritates Jenny. Jenny frustrates Carol. Carol belittles John. John fancies Nadia. Leaving work for the day, the four co-workers become trapped in an elevator. *Write the scene!*

010. High Time

Two characters sit side by side, dangerously close to the edge of a motorway bridge. As traffic zooms by below them, one character is moved to share a life-altering secret with the other. *Write the scene!*

011. Coffee with Cathy

CATHY (*choking on her cappuccino*). That's so embarrassing! I'd have died.

LINDA. I wanted to.

CATHY. How did she even begin to explain that?

Write the scene!

012. Last Train

A fight between two gangs breaks out on the last train of the evening. Caught in the crossfire are a pensioner and a thirteen-year-old. If they stay silent or try to move carriages, they risk becoming a target or getting caught in the brawl. If they get off, they have no means of getting home without a long walk in the dark. *Write the scene!*

013. So... This is Goodbye

In a very public place, two characters say a very private goodbye. *Write the scene!*

014. Looking Out

Looking out of the window of your writing space, the bus, the train, or wherever you are. What are the first two things you see? Write them down, along with the two most prominent colours. Finally, if you were to open the window, what two sounds would you hear? Use the snapshot information you have noted down to write a six-line scene (or poem, ditty or story). *Give it a go!*

015. Ethel

Ethel sits in a rocking chair in the kitchen, unseen by Martin, who returns with grocery shopping. He closes the door and unpacks the shopping.

> ETHEL. I folded the laundry and put a rice pudding in the oven. Should be done in an hour, love.
>
> MARTIN. I'm sorry… who are you?

Write the scene!

016. Were You in the War?

Waiting for his father to pay for groceries, eight-year-old Daniel sits beside a decorated army veteran on a supermarket bench and strikes up a conversation. *Write the scene!*

017. Donna's Kitchen

Donna and Jean are elderly sisters. Donna is jealous of Jean. Jean thinks Donna is full of herself. They are in Donna's kitchen, making a cake. *Write the scene!*

018. Mum?

Cindy visits her mother's grave on the first anniversary of her death. She replaces the withered flowers and lights a candle. Through tears, Cindy speaks to her mother, updating her on the past year. *Write the scene!*

019. I Should… Probably…

After their work Christmas party, Ben and Ruby end up in bed together. The next morning, blinding sunlight and the smell stale cigarette smoke provide a harsh wake-up. This was a mistake. They both know it, and they both want to leave. Still naked, neither wants to make the first move. *Write the scene!*

020. Confession Time

Taking his seat inside the confessional, a priest has something he needs to get off his chest. Surprised to find the tables turned, a parishioner listens as the priest repents. *Write the scene!*

021. Always the Bridesmaid

At her best friend's wedding reception, a very single and very inebriated Harriet staggers across to the DJ and picks up the microphone. Bringing the dancefloor to an abrupt standstill, she has the attention of the entire room. *Write the scene!*

022. It was a Good Year

Feeling out of his depth at a high-brow function, Miles nods along as his work chums enthuse about a vintage bottle of Rioja. As they discuss the acidity, tannins and body of the wine, Miles plays it safe and offers praise for the hints of cherry which he figures are present in most reds. When asked to elaborate, his lack of wine knowledge forces him to improvise. *Write the scene!*

023. Fuelled by Love

Filling up at the gas station late at night, two drivers catch each other's eyes across an empty forecourt. What if this is love at first sight? They both feel something. Are they really going to let each other drive off into the night? *Write the scene!*

024. Too Much Information

Riding home from work on the bus, Janet speaks to her friend Alison on the phone, bringing her up to speed on a very personal medical condition. For the other passengers on the bus, this is way too much information. *Write the scene!*

025. Coffee?

Taking fresh towels to the guest bathroom, a mother accidentally walks in on her son's wife, Ruth, who is showering. Once dressed, Ruth joins her husband and his mortified mother for breakfast. *Write the scene!*

026. Family Dinner

Three members of the same family sit down to dinner. Show by the things they say to one another that one is a control freak, one a pathological liar, and one a narcissist. *Write the scene!*

027. Misguided Tour

It's Emily's first day as an open-top-bus tour guide. As her coach departs with a group of Italian college students, she realises that she has forgotten to bring her folder of notes. With her mind completely blank, the students and their teacher have lots of questions. *Write the scene!*

028. Rat-trap

Use the following line from *Of Mice and Men* (John Steinbeck) to inspire an original scene between a mother and son: 'Well, you keep away from her, cause she's a rat-trap if I ever seen one.' *Write the scene!*

029. Dog's Dinner

Late at night on a quiet subway train, a passenger with a dog opens a can of dog food straight onto the carriage floor. A well-heeled couple travelling home from a theatre trip sit opposite. *Write the scene!*

030. A Hampered Heist

After holding up a bank at gunpoint, Max makes a run for it with a rucksack full of cash. However, as he scrambles to leave, he trips over one of the customers he has instructed to lay on the floor, breaking his leg! Waiting outside, his getaway driver sees this through the doors and drives away. *Write the scene!*

031. How Many Children, Madam?

A middle-aged woman stands at the counter of a children's soft play centre in her socks, holding her shoes. She is alone.

PLAYWORKER. How many children, Madam?

Write the scene!

032. Good Kitty. Bad Kitty

In a pet store: he wants a cat; she does not. There is only one cat left. It has fleas. Lots of fleas. *Write the scene!*

033. Pineapples

In the fruit and veg aisle of a busy supermarket, a persistent customer has a plethora of questions about the sourcing, importing, sustainability, harvesting and growing methods of the Costa Rican pineapples on sale. The unlucky store assistant is short of knowledge, time and patience. *Write the scene!*

034. Two Men and Their…

A man sits on a bench by the harbour, sharing his ice cream with a most unusual pet. After a moment, another man with an equally unique pet joins him. *Write the scene!*

035. Hey! Wait Up!

Riding the bus home from work, a man spots a friend walking by whom he hasn't seen for years. He pushes the stop button and rushes to catch up to his friend. Placing his hand on the man's shoulder, he realises this is not his friend. *Write the scene!*

036. What Happened?

Brushing his teeth in front of the bathroom mirror on the eve of his fiftieth birthday, Graham catches sight of himself. The years have crept up on him. When did his hair turn grey? When did those wrinkles below his eyes appear? He stops brushing and takes a moment to catch up with himself. *Write the scene!*

037. Blind Date

Sadie is single. She reluctantly agrees to go on a blind date organised by her friend – assured that the mystery man is a perfect match for her. However, as the waitress leads Sadie to her waiting date, it is immediately apparent that he is anything but. *Write the scene!*

038. I'm So Happy for You

Following their auditions for the same character in a daytime medical drama, best friends Bella and Alicia are having coffee when Bella's agent calls. She didn't get the role. Straight after, Alicia's agent calls with good news. *Write the scene!*

039. No Escaping the Past

Aaron's family are ready for a fresh start, having left the horrors of the past behind them and moved to a new town. However, as Aaron sits down for class on his first day at a new college, another student decides to search for Aaron online.

STUDENT. Hey, Aaron…

Write the scene!

040. Pound of Bananas

At an East End fruit and veg stall, elderly grocers Brenda and Alice have amassed quite an audience, with calls to witness the weight-loss powers of their miracle banana diet. The crowd are intrigued. *Write the scene!*

041. More Wine?

Wanting to get ahead at work, Greg invites his unyielding boss and her wife to the home he shares with his girlfriend Jennine for dinner. Helping everyone to relax, Jennine keeps the wine flowing. However, Greg is on edge. Jennine tends to drink too much and has a history of saying exactly what she thinks… no filter. *Write the scene!*

042. Lock the Door!

Use this line from *Cat on a Hot Tin Roof* (Tennessee Williams) to inspire an original scene between a pub landlord, his barmaid, Maggie, and a patron: 'Maggie, we're through with lies and liars in this house. Lock the door.' *Write the scene!*

043. Cat Whisperer

Concerned that their cat Daisy has become reclusive, Tom and Ellie take her to see a feline therapist. Listening to the cat, the therapist becomes deeply embarrassed when Daisy shares a very private and slightly awkward secret about her owners that is troubling her. *Write the scene!*

044. That's Her!

Distressed, Veronica rushes into a busy post office, followed by two police officers. She leads them towards a mother with two small children at a cashier's window.

VERONICA. That's her!

Write the scene!

045. Did You Pack the Case Yourself, Sir?

When an elderly airline passenger struggles to carry her luggage, she asks a young man to help her through security. However, when the case is pulled aside for further inspection by officials, the old lady is nowhere to be seen. *Write the scene!*

046. Poor Nick

A woman visits her parents to tell them she and her husband, Nick, are getting a divorce. She is anxious with good reason. Her parents love Nick and immediately take his side. *Write the scene!*

047. Captive Audience

Three prisoners share a cell… but not a sense of humour. One man tells a joke or two. How do the other two react? *Write the scene!*

217

048. A Novel Approach

Novelist Lindy is browsing the shelves of her local bookstore for inspiration. As she moves in to pick up a book of interest, another customer steps right in front of her and takes it. After tutting, Lindy quickly recoils as she realises that the customer is none other than her all-time favourite author. *Write the scene!*

049. Mother Undercover

A concerned mother is worried that her daughter is involved in some sort of trouble. She decides to follow her on a trip into town, but what she observes is even more shocking than she could ever have imagined. *Write the scene!*

050. Grace

William brings his girlfriend, Chloë, to a family dinner for the first time. As is the family tradition, William's mother asks Chloë if she would like to say grace before the family eat. Caught on the back foot, non-religious Chloë leads the family in a truly unique blessing. *Write the scene!*

051. Marriage Guidance

Use the following line from *Three Tall Women* (Edward Albee) to inspire an original scene between a couple and their marriage guidance counsellor: 'That's the happiest moment. When it's all done. When we stop. When we can stop.' *Write the scene!*

052. Double Trouble

Losing his phone and wallet on a night out at an illegal rave, Lewis decides to call his own number. A woman answers, speaking only to give an address which Lewis scribbles down. Deciding not to involve the police due to his whereabouts at the time of the theft, Lewis goes to the address. *Write the scene!*

053. An Important Message

Three missionaries visit Valerie's home on a Sunday morning. She would usually turn them away and close the door immediately. However, for some reason, today, she decides to listen to what they have to say. *Write the scene!*

054. Uber Annoying

After a long flight, Magda takes a taxi home. She is exhausted and just wants to get home quickly… and quietly. However, her driver has other ideas and will not stop talking. *Write the scene!*

055. Quick! The Vegans are Coming

Lights up on dairy farmer Carys, who reads aloud a newspaper headline, 'Veganism to Become UK Law'. *Write the scene!*

056. Beans

Disillusioned with life, Andrea sits down for tea with husband, Gary. He presents her with a plate of baked beans on toast and tucks in. Andrea pushes the beans around her plate.

ANDREA. We need to talk.

Write the scene!

057. Sorry... You Were Saying?

On a dull dinner date, Luke's eyes are wandering. As his date talks at length about workplace politics, Luke is locked in a flirtatious gaze with the barmaid standing behind her. *Write the scene!*

058. D'oh!

A Chicago cop sits in his parol car with a cup of black coffee and a glazed doughnut. With each bite he takes, he recites a eulogy for the dearly departing dough. *Write the scene!*

059. Last Orders

As a barman takes stock at the end of the night, a sorry-looking man stares into his glass, nursing the last few drops of scotch. In a drunken stupor, the man admits to an unbelievable crime. Does the barman take notice, or ignore the drunken confession? *Write the scene!*

060. The Thing is...

Stephen takes pity on Darren, a junior co-worker who has just broken up with his girlfriend, and invites Darren to stay with him for a couple of nights. However, ten days later, Darren is still there. This is awkward for Stephen, but he decides to act. *Write the scene!*

061. Held to Account

Use this line from *Topdog/Underdog* (Suzan-Lori Parks) to inspire an original scene between a politician and a disgruntled constituent: 'You're only yourself when no one's watching!' *Write the scene!*

062. Strip Search

A police officer approaches the driver-side window of a vehicle he has just pulled over for driving at twice the speed limit. After asking the occupants to step out of the car, he glances down to see that the driver and three passengers are all totally naked. *Write the scene!*

063. Sam's Sonnet

Tom says something which includes an unusual or funny word. Inspired by this word, Sam improvises a short poem. Is Tom impressed? Is he direct or indirect with his feedback? *Write the scene!*

064. This is Not Goodbye

As her beloved poodle lies on the vet's table, a heartbroken woman says goodbye for the very last time. However, just as the vet is about to administer the drug that will euthanise the pooch, something unexpected happens. *Write the scene!*

065. Wrong Place. Wrong Time

Rex waits in his car outside of the post office for his wife. After a moment, a man wearing a balaclava and carrying a rucksack opens the passenger door and threatens Rex to drive. *Write the scene!*

066. Three's a Crowd

Burning the midnight oil, a writer struggles to move two characters forwards following a reconciliation scene. Talking out loud to them, she finds herself caught in the middle and struggles to avoid taking sides. *Write the scene!*

067. French Fury

On the last night of a romantic weekend away in Paris, David tells his girlfriend Louise that he has something important to ask her. As David kneels, Louise begins to cry. David proceeds to fasten his shoelace whilst asking Louise if she would be able to look after his dog Bruno whilst he and his mates go on a 'lads weekend' to Dublin. David stands, surprised to find his girlfriend in tears. *Write the scene!*

068. Sandwiches

Use this line from *The Odd Couple* (Neil Simon) to inspire an original scene between a downbeat deli owner and their customer: 'I got brown sandwiches and green sandwiches. It's either very new cheese or very old meat.' *Write the scene!*

069. Sext Scene

Use the last text message you received as the first line of dialogue in a scene between a conservative librarian, and an elderly reader in search of erotic fiction. *Write the scene!*

070. Can I Tell You Something?

A man sits on a park bench with a knife in his hand. After a moment, an elderly lady sits next to him. She spots the blade but is not alarmed. Her calmness and ability to listen and empathise cause a reversal. *Write the scene!*

071. Photo Booth

Sitting inside a passport photo booth, a woman starts to sob uncontrollably. Waiting outside, another woman hears her crying. The waiting woman attempts to comfort the stranger.

WOMAN. I don't like having my photo taken either.

Write the scene!

072. Lice!

As a group of parents wait outside of a school classroom to collect their children, a teacher emerges with a pile of letters relating to an outbreak of headlice. When the teacher requests parents inspect their children's hair, one parent becomes defensive. *Write the scene!*

073. Tongue Thai-ed

During a break on a business trip to Bangkok, Bianca sips Prosecco with her friend Sheila in a nail bar. Bianca makes several nasty comments about her nail technician, who she assumes can't understand what she is saying. *Write the scene!*

074. Socks Reunited

Right Sock has been through the laundry cycle. Left Sock was left in the sock drawer. After three days apart, they are finally reunited. Have the socks been pining for each other? Or has Left Sock already been paired up with a new Right Sock? *Write the scene!*

075. A Stranger's Touch

Riding on a crowded train, a man is surprised, but not opposed or offended, when a stranger randomly holds his hand. *Write the scene!*

076. I'll Be Right Back

Having invited a life-insurance salesman into his home, eighty-year-old Russell soon realises that he is being taken for a ride. Offering to make some coffee for the scammer, Russell briefly leaves the room, with a plan to take matters into his own hands. *Write the scene!*

077. You ##&%#@*!!!

Rock-music fans Mike and Molly are sitting on a porch drinking beer. They are arguing over which is the better band, Led Zeppelin or Pink Floyd? They have a heated debate… without using traditional swear words. Get creative! *Write the scene!*

078. Flight of Fear

As the in-flight service begins on a long-haul flight from London to Singapore, a woman lowers her tray table to find a handwritten warning note from the previous passenger. *Write the scene!*

079. Loose Chippings

Use this line from *Pat and Margaret* (Victoria Wood) to inspire an original scene between a bitter children's ballet teacher and her former student, now a principal dancer at the Royal Ballet: 'Life's not fair, is it? Some of us drink Champagne in the fast lane, and some of us eat our sandwiches by the loose chippings on the A597.' *Write the scene!*

080. A Mermaid's Tail

On a whaling ship off the coast of Norway, a group of fisherman reel in their net to discover that they have caught a mermaid. What do they do? *Write the scene!*

081. Cold Feet

A mother and daughter are in a changing room, before a floor-length mirror. The mother is thrilled about this wedding, whilst the daughter is tempted to call the wedding off! Have the characters state their feelings, through tone, gesture and indirect comments. *Write the scene!*

082. Never Meet Your Idols

A music fan wins tickets for a VIP 'meet and greet' with their life-long hero. Escorted backstage before the concert, they wait nervously in the green room for the music legend to arrive. After a long wait, the meeting gets underway, and things seem to be going well. However, when the star's assistant leaves the room, they make an unusual request of their fan. *Write the scene!*

083. Anyone Home?

In darkness except for a porch light, the teenagers step gently across a carpet of fallen leaves and approach the door of what they assume is a derelict house. Before they have a chance to reach up and pull the rusted bell chain… the door opens. *Write the scene!*

084. Detour!

After collecting a man and a woman from a hotel, a ride-sharing driver overhears a conversation so concerning that he decides to take a detour via the police station. The couple knows the city well and questions the route, how does he hold his nerve and keep his cool? *Write the scene!*

085. What Was That?

At four-thirty in the morning, Jenny sits bolt upright in bed. She is sure she heard a loud clatter downstairs in the kitchen. Terrified, she holds her breath, listening anxiously. She hears the noise again. *Write the scene!*

086. Short Bark and Sides

Recently released from prison after serving time for slitting the throat of one of his customers, a barber struggles to find work. When he takes a job as a dog groomer, his next customer has a nose for retribution, and proves to be even more bloodthirsty than he is! *Write the scene!*

087. Thief!

After paying for his coffee, a man drops his small change into the tip jar on the counter. A moment later, as he waits for his drink, the lady behind him is a few cents short for her order. He takes one of the coins he put into the tip jar and gives it to her. Someone else in the queue notices this and calls 'Thief'! *Write the scene!*

088. Reset Password

Tina and Ross have just started dating. They are discussing online security. What happens when they each reveal one of their passwords to the other? Her password? iH8M3N (I hate men). *Write the scene!*

089. Speak Now…

As a bride and groom-to-be hold hands at the altar, a voice, unknown to the couple, calls out from the pews when the priest asks for any objections. *Write the scene!*

090. Yak for Sale

Speaking on the phone to the advertising department at her local newspaper, Gloria reads aloud an advert for the sale of her Tibetan yak. She explains how she came to own the yak, why he makes a great pet, and why she is selling him. *Write the scene!*

091. Something Fishy

Returning home from school, Leah and Sophia are concerned that their goldfish Monty looks… 'funny'. Their father assures them that he's fine, avoiding the fact that the fish in the tank is a replacement for Monty, who was found floating on the top of the water shortly after the girls left for school. *Write the scene!*

092. Closet Case

With the children sleeping, a nosy babysitter starts to investigate her employer's home. As she opens a closet in the master bedroom, what she discovers makes her immediately regret her decision to snoop. *Write the scene!*

093. Battenberg

Use this line from *A Doll's House* (Henrik Ibsen) to inspire an original scene between two members of a Women's Institute as they set up for a bake sale: 'You arranged everything according to your own taste, and so I got the same tastes as you – or else I pretended to. I am really not quite sure which – I think sometimes the one and sometimes the other.' *Write the scene!*

094. The Diplomatic Dressmaker

At a fitting for her bridesmaid dress, curvy Cathy is insistent that the dressmaker fit her for a dress two sizes smaller than her actual size. *Write the scene!*

095. Pumpkin Pie

David hasn't seen Diana for over seven years, since she walked out on him on their wedding night, before emptying their joint bank account. It's 10 p.m. There's a knock at the door. It's Diana, and she presents David with a freshly baked pumpkin pie. *Write the scene!*

096. An Uninvited Guest

Angie has noticed strange things happening in her home for the last few weeks. Items going missing, footsteps in empty rooms, flickering lights, food vanishing from the refrigerator, and appliances with minds of their own. As she sits alone on the sofa watching a late-night talk show, an elderly lady in a nightdress sits down next to her and changes the channel. *Write the scene!*

097. Photographic Evidence

Whilst clearing out her late mother's house, Celia finds a disposable camera and decides to have the film developed. Collecting the photos, she discovers a secret that alters everything she thought she knew about her family and herself. *Write the scene!*

098. Blackmail

Fired from his job, Grant turns up at his ex-boss's house late at night, threatening to reveal a damaging company secret to the press if he is not reinstated. *Write the scene!*

099. Horror Scope

Flicking through the Sunday papers, Anthea turns to the horoscopes to find out what the coming week has in store for Sagittarius. It reads: 'Stop whatever you are doing and leave town immediately. Disastrous repercussions await those who decide to tempt fate.' Anthea puts down the newspaper and turns to her husband. *Write the scene!*

100. Room Service?

Morgan is a lawyer at a top New York law firm. Travelling for business, she checks in to her hotel room after a hectic day of back-to-back meetings. As she sits on the edge of the bed and kicks off her shoes, a man comes out of the bathroom, fresh from the shower with a towel around his waist. *Write the scene!*

101. Smells Like Love

On their third date, Dale cooks dinner for Sukie. Show by the way she compliments his cooking and describes the aromas in the kitchen that she has fallen head over heels in love with him. *Write the scene!*

Tried all 101 quick-fire prompts?

How about trying them again in a different genre? Why not see how a prompt plays out as a scene from a thriller versus a romantic comedy; or as a slice of dystopian fantasy instead of naturalism?

You could experiment further by switching up your writing environment to see if this inspires different results. Does writing to different background music make a difference? Perhaps smooth jazz inspires a different response to K-pop or classic rock? How about writing early in the morning versus the last thing at night? What about writing outside in natural light compared to writing under the glare of your desk lamp? You might even try writing with a fountain pen instead of typing.

Have fun and mix things up to write a totally original scene every time.

PART EIGHT

SAVASANA AFTER WRITING

I spoke at the beginning of the book about introducing mindful meditation into my practice, before sitting down to write. This part of the book describes how to introduce Savasana at the end of a writing session.

Savasana, pronounced 'shah-VAH-sah-nah', is sometimes referred to as the 'corpse pose', and is often used at the end of a yoga class to aid relaxation, promote calmness of the mind, and rejuvenate the body. During Savasana, as your breath deepens, any stresses from the day are forgotten as you surrender all effort, worry and thoughts, slipping into a peaceful and blissful reflective state.

Just as a yoga instructor will encourage students to take a moment at the end of each class to recognise all that they have achieved, I think it is important to acknowledge and reward the progress that we make in each and every writing session, feeling fulfilled and energised to resume work next time.

8.1

Savasana

Savasana presents a rare opportunity at the end of your writing session to enjoy a moment of calm, stillness and tranquillity.

Start, if possible, by dimming the lights in your space, or closing all blinds or curtains. As with the mindful meditation practice (see pages 3–9), you may also like to light some candles and play gentle music. If you search 'Savasana' on Spotify, you will find numerous ready-to-go playlists. If you have a yoga mat, lay it out on the floor; otherwise, a towel or just the carpet will suffice. A few drops of lavender oil on a small hand towel to place over your eyes will help to calm and comfort you.

Now that your space is set, lie down on your back and use a pillow or a folded towel to support your head. Next, bring your feet as wide as your mat and let them flop open. Relax your arms a few inches away from your body, palms facing the sky. Close your eyes and make any final adjustments so that you are entirely comfortable. Once you begin Savasana, try just to be. Avoid moving your hands or fidgeting, as the deeper you relax, the greater the benefit.

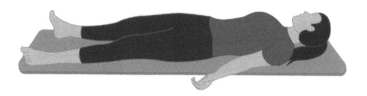

Now… breathe naturally.

Once you feel relaxed and settled, take a deep inhalation of breath. As you do so, your chest will expand, and your body will gently lift. As you exhale, notice how your body melts back into the floor. Imagine a feather gently stroking your body from head to toe. As it passes over your face and sweeps across your body, it removes any residual tension and allows you to feel completely relaxed, safe and at ease in this pose. Allow your eyes to become heavy, and your tongue to fall away from the roof of your mouth. On each inhalation, feel your body lift, and on each exhalation, allow the body to relax deeply, sinking into the ground.

Surrender to the pose for several minutes, letting go of the pressure of submission deadlines, word-count targets, or pending redrafts. As a thought comes into your mind, let it drift away, remaining in the present moment. Back to your state of total relaxation. Focus simply on breathing deeply, in… and out.

Today was wonderful. You have written; therefore, you have progressed. Relax and take this time to acknowledge all that you have achieved in your session. Writing begins with a blank page; today you put words on that page and created something that did not exist before you started.

Reawaken

After about ten minutes, or whenever you feel ready to leave the pose, keeping your eyes closed, begin to reawaken your body by slowly starting to wiggle your fingers and toes. Gently move your head from side to side, slowly reawakening yourself, pointing and flexing your toes and stretching your arms above your head.

In your own time, on a deep exhale, bring your knees into your chest and roll onto one side, curling your body into a fetal position. After a moment, return to your back and then slowly into a seated pose with your spine sitting tall, your legs crossed and hands rested on your knees.

After a moment, place your hands together in front of your heart and bow your head.

SAVASANA

When you are ready, slowly open your eyes and take a moment to notice how you feel having completed your practice. You made a choice today, not only to dedicate time to your writing, but in making time to restore and replenish your mental and spiritual wellbeing. Take this peaceful energy with you as you go through the rest of your day…

And stay inspired.

ALPHABETICAL INDEX OF EXERCISES

www.nickhernbooks.co.uk

facebook.com/nickhernbooks

twitter.com/nickhernbooks